This book is due for return on or before the last date shown above but it may be renewed by personal application, post, or telephone, quoting this date and the book number.

HERTFORDSHIRE COUNTY LIBRARY
COUNTY HALL, HERTFORD.

L.32

The
Collected Poems of
ROY CAMPBELL
VOLUME 2

The
Collected Poems of
ROY CAMPBELL

VOLUME 2

The Bodley Head
London

Printed in Great Britain for
THE BODLEY HEAD LTD
10 Earlham Street, London WC2
by The Camelot Press Ltd, Southampton
Set in Monotype Centaur
First published 1957
Reprinted 1961

Dedicated to Rob Lyle

CONTENTS

Later Poems
(1939-1956)

PREFACE

For PERMISSION to include several poems in this book from *Talking Bronco* I thank Messrs. Faber & Faber. Owing to considerations of space and printing some of my published poems are held over for Volume III of my *Collected Poems*, which I hope to publish soon. To Mr. C. J. Sibbett I owe the rescue from the Cape Town archives of the only surviving fragment of "The Golden Shower", a poem of some two thousand five hundred lines, which I lost at sea in 1926, and which, but for the diligence of my old friend, would have disappeared entirely. This poem followed "The Flaming Terrapin" but preceded most of the African poems in "Adamastor" and "The Wayzgoose". Though I have just re-written and overhauled this poem from stem to stern, I have preserved both its mood and tense, written as it was in the pagan paradise of my childhood, boyhood, and early manhood, while living as a hunter, a fisherman, and a whaler in the bush of Natal and Zululand, and on the Indian Ocean. Other poems, reprinted herein, appeared in the following papers and reviews. *The Catacomb, Nine, Nimbus, Poetry London-New York, The American National Review, The English National Review, The South African Nation, The Tablet, The Northern Review, The Outspan, The New Statesman, Adam* and certain publications of the Middle East and East African Commands such as *Jambo* and *Off Parade*. I thank the Editors for permission to reprint them here.

The poems in this volume are arranged by me in order, unlike those in the first volume, some of which, owing to my absence abroad, appeared under the wrong headings.

Though forming a whole poem in itself, "The Vision of our Lady over Toledo" really belongs to my long Epic poem *Flowering Rifle* and is here printed with it.

I must here admit the theft in "The Rodeo" of the phrase "star-clovered" from Rob Lyle's "Guitar", in compensation for which I dedicate this book to his, as yet, undiscovered genius.

Early Poems
(1926-1939)

Jousé's Horses
(*To Frédéric Mistral, Neveu*)

Coasting the delta of the dead lagoons,
The patron said "We're in for dirty weather.
See, here come Jousé's horses, all together,
(Confound the vermin!) making for the dunes."

And there along the low verge of the land
All silver fire, (Niagara set free!)
A hundred silken streamers swept the sand,
And with them came the wind, and rose the sea!

★

Canidia and Priapus
(*Adapted from Horace's Satire*)

When old Canidia ghosted on the prowl
To serenade you with her grisly choir,
Whose trombone is the toad, whose flute the owl,
And jingled wealth her soul—destructive lyre:
Presenting arms, the sentry of the garden,
With resolute backfire, I dinned the night,
Whose thunder served our slack morale to harden,
Reversing all the gears of her delight.
That thunder was the sacred power of verse
That bowed her towering Castle with its curse
And to the peering rabble gave the keep:
While with such ridicule it struck her charms

13

The nymphs ran screaming from her outstretched arms
While she retired in Solitude to weep.

★

Fragment from "The Golden Shower"
(To Mary Campbell)

Amphibious to this world of sunlit hours
And to that other which is only ours,
But whose divine realities in this,
As stars in pools, their own reflections kiss,
While here beneath a roof of cloudless days
We lovers, loitering in the forest ways,
Heedless of how the doting world may turn
Make it our wisest study to unlearn
Its idle cants, forgetting them so far
That for this brighter sphere in which we burn
Astronomers might name another star—
May Love, whose quick philosophers we are,
Our hearts of their mortality absolve,
Shatter the old inherited ideal
Round which men's outworn energies revolve
Like spokes of wood or dull, mechanic steel,
And forge in us new weapons for assault
On all that is established in men's hearts
That into swifter saddles we may vault
Remastering the great forgotten arts
By which men rose above the brutes of old,
Before they wearied of their steep ascent,
Anchored their spirits to a load of gold
And with a slack humility unbent
To teach themselves a vegetable growth;
We shall recapture the brave force they used
In their steep uprush, ere this finer sloth
Was like the sap of cabbages infused.
Destroying in ourselves the dreaming past,
Repealing our allegiance to its laws,
We shall defeat our memory at last,
And with new strength, unhingeing silver claws,

Leap on the mountain-backed unwieldy Lie
Under whose tyranny men crawl and die—
Thus like two lions we shall ride elate
That on a giant buffalo, in state,
Ride through their forest-kingdom breathing fire
To pitch their quarry headlong in the mire.
So by our bold example we may found
A dynasty of lovers in this land,
Where grunting faction makes the only sound,
Where clanking fetters ring on every hand,
Where slaves by slaves more servile are compelled,
And naught, save paunches, in respect are held:
So by our bold example we may found
A princely line, fore-run a titan race
That by their strength and beauty shall be crowned
More royally than kings: and they shall trace
Their birth from us and learn like us to move
Through cities with a bold insulting grace
Clashing bright spurs: their beauty will reprove
The hucksters of the counter-jumping race,
And with our likeness tease their sullen scowls,
Like sunrays to the noon-afflicted owls
Smiting their blank inquiry in the face.
Is our young brutal loveliness enough—
Her laughing breasts or my horse-taming strength?
Should we not in less perishable stuff
Take measurements, that it may go the length
Of our life's journey, clothe us but so far
Into the country of the evening star
As to where lovers bid their last good-bye,
And there, cast off, like some rich garment lie,
From which our heirs-in-love their own may tear
And in our stead as regal emblems wear?
Then let us now, in our strong youthful prime,
Invest our riches in one blaze of rhyme—
And so to our old age and airy ghosts
Bequeath the memories of our shining feats,
That, when they reach those shadow-peopled coasts,
They still may buckle on as lordly boasts
Wherewith to swagger in those mournful streets.

15

Even as the Sea, coloured with boastful hues,
Into whose gloom the dancing stars diffuse
Their flatteries of fire, and seem to shake
A thousand sleeping Arguses awake—
All glittering with fierce hypnotic eyes,
Extravagantly vaunts his gorgeous dyes,
Flaunting his pride against the barren shores
Careless of whom his flaring lights amaze,
Though it be but to startle grunting boars,
Or bloodshot, staring buffaloes to daze—
So I whose mind love fires with glancing rays
Would vie with peacocks and, around the globe
Fantailing forth a mesh of coloured rhyme,
Would weave for my young love a fitting robe
With which to shimmer in the winds of time,
Teaching men's hearts a mutinous commotion
As it waves forth to undiscovered lands,
Tigered with gold and azure like the ocean,
And braided with the green of palmy strands.
Ghosting like starlight through the minds of men
And panthered with their jealous eyes, as when
The ocean draws the wonder of the skies
And wears the gold amazement of their eyes,
So I would have her beauty glide forever
Glassing its image in that rushing river
Where life unravels into tragic tales
And time flows nightward lit with mortal dreams—
A moon above those serpent-winding streams
That have the eyes of poets for their scales.

Here in this land, where nature unconfined
Taunts the great desert of the human mind
From which as yet no bright euphorbias shoot
But only sweet unwieldy pumpkins fruit,
Vast sprawling platitudes with sugared vein
Cysts of the mind, and tumours of the brain:
Where Poesy has ever, on weak knees,
Limped in the track of old hypocrisies,
And, like a bullfrog, wheezing grateful cries
Snatched with a nimble flicker of its tongue
The tinsel sweetness of their sugared lies,

Uncaring that the brightest-coloured flies
Are often hatched the deepest in the dung.
Here in this desert, far from any Muse,
(Except yourself, the tenth, most proud and young)
Where Thought, half-starved, like a soft cactus screws
Its squirming root and rears its stunted blade
Scarce high enough to grant a lizard shade—
Here shall I strike my roots whose strenuous thongs
Into the barren lava hour by hour,
Incisively shall drive their eager prongs
And crest the desert boulders with a Flower.
Like a Magnolia with its pollen loaded,
As heavy as the gold on Danae's thigh,
That by its own effulgence is exploded
Into a cloud of fragrance, one long sigh—
So I, whom love exalting to a god,
Forces, a fiery blossom, from the pod
Out of my own morality escape,
And shower, like Jove, to Danae's golden rape:—
And while my words in many a burning gyre
Fume on the breeze and set the winds on fire
Like pollen in the spring; your soul shall seem
A glittering bee that travels to and fro
Loaded with all the wealth that I can dream
And all that I can realize and show.

The drought is done. Now to their gusty games,
Tagging their nimble heels with fleeter flames
Than those with which they charred the winter grass,[1]
The winds upon the tops of lilies pass.
New sources rimple from the mountain-roots
And drawn in silver leashes by the spruits
Long files of red-gold lilies wind and meet
To spoor the rovings of their crystal feet:
The marshes, where the yellow weavers breed,
Whirr with great gusts of gold, and as they swing,
Shrill on the bending rushes, every reed
Lights its frail taper with a burnished wing.

[1] This refers to the annual (and suicidal) burning of the grass throughout Africa by the natives.

Here, where relumed by changing seasons, burn
The phoenix trees of Africa in turn,
Each from the other's ashes taking fire
As swiftly to revive as to expire,
Mimosa, jacaranda, kaffirboom,
And tulip-tree, igniting bloom from bloom,
While through their zodiac of flowery signs
The flame-furred sun like some huge moth is whirled
Circling forever, as he fades or shines,
Around the open blossom of the world —
All things as if to Venus' touch ignite
And the grey soil is tinder to her tread
Whence married flowers explode into the light —
And burn with fiery pollen as they wed.
She burns through bark and wood as flame through glass
The dust is fuel to her warm desire
On which, with scintillating plumes, the grass
Runs waving like a disembodied fire:
But we of all her splendours are most splendid
In whom the rest are held and comprehended,
And our clear sprites, whom rays and showers begem,
Burn through each other as the world through them.

Though we seem merely mortal, what we are,
Is clearly mirrored on a deathless flood.
We change and fade: our dust is strewn afar —
Only the ancient river of our blood,
Rising far-off in unimagined spaces,
Red with the silt and ruin of the past
And churning with the strife of savage races,
Like deep Zambezi goes on rolling past,
Swiftens through us its energies unending,
And reaches out, beneath the shades we cast,
To what vast ocean of the night descending
Or in what sunny lake at last to sleep,
We do not know — save that it turns to foam,
Just here, for us; its currents curl and comb
And all its castalies in thunder leap,
Silvering, forth into a white resilience
Of ecstacy, whose momentary brilliance

Must compensate eternities of sleep.
Knowing these things, are not we lovers, then,
Though mortal in our nature, more than men?
Since by our senses, as by rivers, veined,
The hills of primal memory are drained,
And the dim summits of their frosty spars,
Whose tops are nibbled by the grazing stars,
Thawed by the rising noon of our desire,
And fusing into consciousness and fire,
Down through the sounding canyons of the soul
Their rich alluvium of starlight roll.

We bear to future times the secret news
That first was whispered to the new-made earth:
We are like worlds with nations in our thews,
Shaped for delight, and primed for endless birth.
We never kiss but vaster shapes possess
Our bodies: towering up into the skies,
We wear the night and thunder for our dress,
While, vaster than imagination, rise
Two giant forms, like cobras flexed to sting,
Bending their spines in one tremendous ring
With all the starlight burning through their eyes,
Fire in their loins, and on their lips the hiss
Of breath indrawn above some steep abyss.
When, like the sun, our heavenly desire
Has turned this flesh into a cloud of fire
Through which our nerves their strenuous lightnings fork,
Eternity has blossomed in an hour
And as we gaze upon that wondrous flower
We think the world a beetle on its stalk.

Let other folk, in theories sublime,
Spin out men's souls like spider-threads through time:—
Be ours to fill the present with our strength
And rear in height what they spin out in length:
Yet while through us those burning forces smite
To which we are the engines of delight,
Let us not dream that here the end is won
Though we must turn our bodies from the sun

And be ourselves no more: for we are fuel
To deathless fires: about us as we play
Eternal forces, hungry for renewal,
Hurtle their live electrons to the fray.

Clouds, crystals, ferns, the ecstacies of matter,
All the fixed forms of beauty, whereunto
Habituated atoms, when they scatter,
By rays and showers are builded up anew—
All these are rhythms woven from the joy
With which live atoms touch, and kiss, and chime,
Yet through the silent chemistry of time,
Weaving smooth harmonies from change and storm,
Come hankering back to their appointed form
As waves to rhythm, or as words to rhyme.

Two poles of sex the night's vast spaces know,
Like distant whirlpools in the deep revolved,
Round which the currents of the ages flow
And worlds, like spray, are driven and dissolved:
And where their ripples cross, with eddying gyre,
They disentwine from swirling spools of fire
The wheeling systems. As when tides have met,
With currents in opposing orbits set,
Each by the other sucked to swirling hollows,
They spin a million circles on the deep,
Ere each the same smooth orbit finds and follows,
And both upon a single pivot sweep.
Slowly their wheeling boundaries encroach;
The turning heavens stir with their approach,
And suns and planets into motion leap;
Even in us they herald their advances,
Flashing their signal through our sense and sight,
And in the casual meeting of our glances
Their outward ripples intersect in light.

Then let us not as perishable dust
Treat these sound bodies which we hold in trust:
But think of them as messengers that meet
Half way between the proud advance of kings,

Announcing their approach, who come to treat,
In gorgeous conclave, of eternal things:
For we are subjects of two foreign powers
Whose grand alliance time will bring to be—
And to this end the valley burns with flowers
And to this end the morning gilds the sea.

In what wild forms have you explored with me
The myriad labyrinths of earthly lust?
I love to think that as a tall young tree,
Golden with pollen, furred with fiery dust,
I fired my shower of Danae to the gust
Or made a happy pander of the bee:
I love to think that in our primal strength
Two panthers clothed us with a night of stars:
Or, as a stream beneath its nenuphars,
We rippled in the python's flowery length:
Or that within the ocean-cleaving whale
We sent up rainbows in majestic play,
And that I sought you then, amid a hail
Of crackling pearls and cataracting spray,
As now amid a rain of golden words.

Yet through the dust a myriad times must pass,
In gold of lilies and in green of grass,
Or in the conscious flesh that now is ours,
Our swift protean essence of delight—
Until the earth has burned away in flowers
Until the stars have eaten up the night,
And having strung, like beads upon a thread,
The changing forms in which we now appear
We in that shining revelry shall tread
Of which we act the faint rehearsals here . . .
For when that final rosary is told,
He who is still new-born (though none so old)
The still-unchanging Present, fold from fold
Tearing the veil, will prove to us at last
That there was never Future time nor Past,
But that, a mere illusion in each tense,
Time was the mere reflection of events,

To fill up gaps between them in our sense—
Unreal and hollow, like the footworn track
That one who travels leaves behind his back,
Or merely finds between him and his goal!
And that, instead of Time or Space, a sole
Personal *presence* occupies the whole.
When all that was, or shall be, merely *is*
And all existence is self-known in His,
That which we feel today in either sprite,
And which we know in moments of delight
Will then be fixed. If into you I burn
Or both into that All, or each return
Singly into ourselves—all shall be one.
And in our love some part of this is done,
For though He shines by us, it's not to dim
The least existence that exists in Him.

★

Driving Cattle to Casas Buenas

The roller perched upon the wire,
Telegrams running through his toes,
At my approach would not retire
But croaked a greeting as he rose,
A telegraph of solar fire.
Girth-high the poppies and the daisies
To brush the belly of my mule:
The thyme was smoking up God's praises,
The sun was warm, the wind was cool,
The white sierra was the icy
Refrigerator of that noon
And in that air so fresh, so spicy,
So steep, so pale, Toledo's June,
The sun seemed smaller than the moon.
Wading through seas of fire and blood
(I never saw such flowers before)
I said to Apis, "What a cud
To make the bulls of Bashan roar!"
The church, with storks upon the steeple,

And scarcely could my cross be signed,
When round me came those Christian people
So hospitably clean, and kind.
Beans and Alfalfa in the manger—
Alfalfa, there was never such!
And rice and rabbit for the stranger.
Thank you very much!

★

In Memoriam of "Mosquito", my partner in the horse-trade, gipsy of the Lozoya Clan

I never felt such glory
As handcuffs on my wrists.
My body stunned and gory
With toothmarks on my fists:
The triumph through the square,
My horse behind me led,
A pistol at my cutlets
Three rifles at my head:
And four of those Red bastards
To hold one wounded man
To all the staring rabble
Proclaiming thus my clan.
Then in the high grey prison
They threw me on the straw,
And through the grille beside me,
Beyond the bridge, I saw
Our other horse "Gaona",
Across the sand-hills fled
With empty saddle: then I knew,
"Mosquito", you were dead,
And low on the meseta
The sun was turning red.
Across the desert sand-hills
It slowly bled from sight,
And, like a horse, a huge black wind
Fled screaming through the night.

★

Pillion to Talavera
(To a Hiking Britisher)

Jump up behind, you pink, fat Pommie!
And profit by this trotting mule
You've stolen my appearance from me
And made me look an equal fool.

You buy dark specs from the opticians
But I collect such eyewear free.
Assault-guards, cops, and Red milicians
Bestowed these two black eyes on me.

My! it must be a lovely sight
To stare at castles through dim mists
But I am equal to your sleight:
Policemen were my oculists.

The Tcheka issued me this pair
And through their lens I read this sentence —
"Red Spaniards! if you take no care
It will be late for your repentance."

Through dark prophetic rings I stare,
With which I read the future thus —
"The Ninth Crusade is in the air,
But poor old England's missed the bus."

I have to keep my goggles still
And see the world more blue than rose:
But you offsaddle yours at will
That play the jockey to your nose.

This flawless Sun without a fleck
You dare not meet it with your eye,
And so you've caught it round your neck
Like ringworm, or a bolshy tie.

While Britons wear that blood-red halter
And in such blinkers draw her hearse,

Britannia's course will never alter
But rumble on from bad to worse.

Her people too will change their genders
And side so oft with the wrong side
Her victories will prove surrenders
And breed disasters far and wide

Since long before Versailles her tallion
Was plain, by God and Man accurst,
Tell them that my mule's a stallion
When you get home to Sissyhurst.

★

To Mary after the Red Terror

When the anopheles were blithe
And life with fever played the whore:
And Death was plying at his scythe
Like a great oarsman at his oar:

And all along that fearful trip
That scorned the vengeance of the past,
I saw the world, a sinking ship,
As from the summit of its mast:

Dingdonging in the lunar steeple
Of madness, with a wound to nurse,
For food and drink I asked the people
But all they gave me was a curse:

Then when we strays were roped and branded
(A burning cross upon the breast)
And in the old Corral were landed
Survivors of the rinderpest, —

You led me to the feet of Christ
Who threatened me with lifted quirt:
But by its loving fury sliced
I staggered upright from the dirt:

And that is why I do not simper,
Nor sigh, nor whine in my harangue.
Instead of ending with a whimper,
My life will finish with a bang!

★

The Carmelites of Toledo

Of the two Camps, from the beginning,
And long before their tides were hurled,
I knew which would do all the winning
If not as most regards the world,
Though earthly victory might come
As so much backwash, drift, or scum
Its sky-careering wave uncurled.

For in the City built with prayer
The Masters of the joyful science
Had held the ages in defiance,
Whose only study is to dare,
Who hardest on the anvil deal,
And thrive upon the hardest fare
Of all who work in fire and steel.

Their lives had won, at comfort's price,
The temper that Toledo lords,
Over a world of waving swords,
From fierce extremes of fire and ice
Deriving such an edge and brilliance
That to their lightning and resilience
No earthly conquest could suffice.

They sailed upon a sinking deck
Beneath a single Mast and Spar
To colonize this blood-red star
Where states and empires plunge to wreck
And, with the world for their Peru,
To vanquish more with wound and scar
Than ever sword set out to do.

No soul so creeping beneath scorn
But they could file its rankled fetters:
Bawds, drunkards, pimps, and men of letters
Who wish their abject souls unborn,
Subjected to their living radium
Returned, as athletes to the stadium,
Who'd come on creaking stretchers borne.

I did not come to dump my sins,
Which, stronger than a mule, I carried,
To their foul load so blithely married
They could not bring me to my shins
For any trick of thief or strumpet.
I came because I heard the Trumpet
When the mad victory begins!

So a loud ass, to be admired,
With no persuasion from the quirt
And heedless that his load is dirt,
By his own braying pibroch-fired,
Might leap the gate, and brave the scoffer,
And come his services to offer
Where snow-white chargers are required.

But from such eagle towers of pity
Eusebio heard my drab confession
That rumbled like a Red procession
When to the 'Meeting' roars the City
With lifted fist and lungs that bray,
His looks abashed that loud Committee
And sent them muttering on their way.

There, parted from those pistoleros,
I stood alone with what I am
As by a wrecked and burning tram.
The companies of drunken heroes
Whose valour varies with their numbers,
Dispersing, teetered to their slumbers,
And each as harmless as a lamb.

And though their fate I could resist,
That gallowed every workless wreck
To dangle from his lifted fist,
His arm a hangrope to his neck,
When like a clinical exhibit
The gesture of the Walking Gibbet
Has jerked him for the Jews to peck—

Yet, to be pitied from such height,
I felt what whets the frenzy-cursed
To slay these Witnesses the first,
Whose cold-and-hunger-bearing sprite,
To thrice their injuries resigned,
Reproaches and rebukes them worst
For so babooning from their kind:

Which, like a glass in a dark place,
Being so much in league with Light,
Might, glinting on the murderer's face,
Reveal him to his own affright,
Or, with a shimmer on the dirk,
Deflect it from the kind of work
That slinks, offended, from the sight.

Their Church, though poorer than an attic,
Anachronised, and seemed to void
Of meaning all that's Meetingoid,
Or tries to pass for Democratic—
More than the grievances they roar,
Its silence galled them to the core
That was so ageless and ecstatic!

But soon the Hoopoe, changing score,
The crested harbinger of battle,
That shares our life amongst the cattle
And only sings in times of war,
The corposant of coming slaughter,
Was singing by the blood-red water
As scarce in centuries before.

And Nature never lit that shore
Where ghost-white suns, foreboding, sank.
And, mirrored with our horses, drank
The flames of blood and liquid ore,
Where Tagus showed that Sky of skies
To which so many soon would rise,
With flames for feathers, streaming gore.

By every sign the times were known,
Humanity by day benighted,
The flesh defiled, dominion slighted,
Blasphemed the high, majestic throne,
And on each wind the whisper blown—
"The weak are strong in hate united,
Woe to the strong who ride alone!"

To those of Carmel half a stranger,
Their purchase from the farms I'd brought
With veld-flowers as an afterthought
That seemed too lovely for the manger,
And now, when ruin lit the towers,
Beset by death, and tracked with danger,
I could not break that chain of flowers:

But proudlier rode to their doomed door
Than ever, plumed and spurred, before
To thundering pigeon-flights of hands,
When, snowed with talc, cascading pearls,
And forested with jet-blue curls,
A whole Sierra made of girls
Sheered sunward from the bloodlit sands!

But Nero's Circus would have been as
A play, himself a paltry showman,
To this most awful of arenas
That stretched, Sahara to the Roman,
With half-a-million lives to spill,
Where to the howl of worse hyenas
I rode but as an alguazil.

The Carmelites, all terror quelled,
The first of the toreros came
In "clothes of light" whose ghostly flame
Was only of the soul beheld,
To flaunt their crimson one by one:
And Death, in turn, by each was felled
Till valour seemed to fix the sun.

The Taurine Sun, in trancèd swoon,
Who loves to linger over peril
And late through evening skies of beryl
Will stretch a famous afternoon,
Had hung so long upon their valour
As, when the smoke dissolved in pallor,
To seem the chill, belated moon.

His radiant face when last I saw
Eusebio bade me take delight:
His flesh was flame, his blood its light
That sought the fire as fire the straw,
And of his agony so cruel
As ruthlessly devoured the spite
As eager flame devours the fuel.

Small wonder then as trash too earthly
The gunbutts drove me from the pin
They smashed to let such Princes in,
When, too presumptuous, as unworthy,
My carcase for a Crown to barter,
The blows acceding to the Martyr
Rebuffed me for a Harlequin.

In my black mask, with bleeding eyes,
I woke as one for gala dressed,
My scapular beneath my vest
Which only then I learned to prize,
And there, like Romeo, the mad lover,
In the forbidden town, discover
And hold the Loved-One to my breast.

So tenderly to fall enamoured
So late—Oh, what a fool was I
To blunder ignorantly by
Just when the third great Nail was hammered,
The strident spear had gashed the cry,
When dicers for the leavings clamoured,
And blood was streaming down the sky!

The Flood-rush, with their blood to break it,
Now filled the land with fire and slaughter.
The Tagus, that was running water,
Was now alive, if blood could make it
That had not had the time to die:
The town, if rushing flames could take it
Was half rebuilded in the sky—

As now a lunar landscape tells
With craters for its domes and spires,
The architecture of the shells,
The hollow sculpture of the fires,
Where memory, to grope its way,
Must seek in absence and dismay
The landmarks that it most admires.

But ages to this blackened tower
Will harness their momentous race
To find, like Tagus at its base,
A station of electric power
Whose Dynamo and sleepless mill
The Christian world with light may fill
And grind its life-sustaining flour:

Where faith-starved multitudes may quarry
As in a mountain, and be fed.
And well might Hell feel sick and sorry
To see the brown monks lying dead,
Where, as with coarse tarpaulins spread,
Each seemed a fifty-horsepower lorry
That to the troops had brought the Bread!

Their wounds were swords—how bravely worth
The care the angels took to smith them!
We thought they took their victory with them
But they had brought it down to earth,
For it was from their neighbouring spire
The proud Alcazar caught the fire
Which gave that splendour phoenix-birth.

A phoenix from its ash to father,
A greater, in its turn, to sire—
It was to be to the Alcazar
What the Alcazar is to Spain,
And Spain is to the world entire;
Unanimous in blood and fire
A single purpose lit the twain!

★

La Mancha in Wartime
(To C. J. Sibbett)

A land of crosses, in the law's despite,
Where every chance designs a crucifix,
For the cicadas, in their choir of sticks
And for the wider, in the kestrel's flight.
The kestrel, and the stationary mill
That sail-less hangs upon the tide of war,
Had not this one significance before
With which their merest shadow signs the hill.
Where men have waifed the land with fire and steel
Of all it spreads its arms to represent,
Amidst their huge abortion of intent,
That symbol is the only thing that's real.
Where widowed of its sign, all they possessed,
The lonely hamlets semaphore their loss,
As in this next, where, half the waste across
Three giant windmills crucify the West,

Each mule-slow road, beneath a plangent sky
Pursues its destination like a ghost,
A Station of the Cross at every post
In silent repetition filing by
While to each gust, as to an angry blow,
From post to post through leagues of groaning wire,
The tons of metal sound their mournful lyre
Vibrating to a thunderstorm of woe.
The Earth, that patient labourer for blows,
It seems, that brays prophetic from the metal,
Defrauded of the life-sufficing nettle
For promises of corn that never grows:
From whose whacked sides, that can support no more,
Its Maker to the madness cries a halt
Reclaiming from each desecrated vault
The sign that only martyrs can restore;
For in these paths blind pilgrims seem to flee,
And every road's a search to find the Cross,
By nothing more assented than its loss
That towers like midnight and outroars the sea.

★

The Hoopoe

Amongst the crags of thyme and samphire,
The wastes of rosemary and fennel,
Up where the wolves in safety kennel
And by the gipsies' lonely campfire,
And round Toledo's shattered walls,
Where, like a crater in the moon,
The desecrated grandeur sprawls—
Though out of season, pitch, and tune,
All day the boding hoopoe calls.

The fire-bird flits amongst the cattle,
Pronouncing victory or doom,
The flashing corposant of battle,
The torch upon the hero's tomb,

The feathered tomahawk that waves
The bonnet of the redskin braves,
And cries once more his warning cry,
Before the grass has healed the graves
Or yet our open wounds be dry.

The comet of approaching war,
He flashes singing through the land,
And where his fiery crest is fanned
The farmyard poultry cluck no more.
Do cage-bred fowls resent this ranger
Of climes, who is the friend of danger
Yet visits, too, their sunless sky?
Is he not, too, a Southern Stranger
Whose gestures they would modify?—

But who has modified their own!
To have the lowdown from their cross-Fates,
Predicting tons of human phosphates
Imported here in flesh and bone,
When fiercely hooting on my claxon,
Before our impetus was known,
I prophesied to Jew and Saxon
The flower-bed they would lay their backs on,
To fodder for our horses grown!

Did I conceal the yawn of loss
They crazed their Gadarene to fly at—
Their Chaos by our solar Fiat,
Their Red Hell foundered by the Cross?—
When long before the bird was singing,
My cattle-whoop and whip were ringing
To head them, if I could, from harm,
Who to our knees for mercy clinging
Would have us exorcise the charm.

So, when the crazed herds rush the canyon,
Converging to the fearful jam,
One rider, their sole sane companion
May race his warning shots to slam,

Desisting as their spate grows thicker
While lifted tails revolve and flicker
Like froth-suds on their frenzied flood,
Till ribs and horns, like crumpled wicker,
And beeves are crushed, like grapes of blood.

Are these the thanks their friends have shown us—
To have me outlawed, gagged, and tied?—
When shouldering a thankless onus,
I blazed the warning far and wide,
Deserving, rather, of a bonus
For vigilance, than bards who lied,
For butchers' bribes, to foolish readers,
And were the rustlers, and stampeders,
And contrabanders in their hide.

With cheap Utopian bait a fisher,
A Market-Angler with the Pen,
Did I ensnare the raw militia
Before they had the sense of men?
Was I the one to bomb their hearse
With saurian millstones, tear by tear,
And then anthologise their verse
To feed the huge wolf-bellied purse
He hugged, so safely, in the rear?

Did I the good cabestro sham,
A King's gold medal round my neck,
Like some sleek bell-decoying ram,
To clank my bookfans to their wreck?
Did I in Mayfair have my fling
And traffic in the slaughtered youth
Who might have lived to serve their King?
Or was I there to prove my truth,
(I think so!) where the bullets sing?

I like this Sergeant of the Birds
With three white chevrons on his wings.
He knows that deeds say more than words
But on the battlefield he sings—

35

While birds who fatten on the dead
And farm the carnage from behind
For gold or offal—cower in dread:
Poets, the vultures of the mind,
And those by nature born and bred.

For when the War-Cloud forks their sky,
They'll seek Utopias oversea,
To jobs in ministries they'll fly,
And funk-holes in the B.B.C.
Where, snugly pocketing the kitty,
They'll sell their pale commercial pity,
In posh editions, for us mere
Shock-workers of the Camp and City
Whose sweat, and life-blood, is their beer.

Before me as the hoopoe cries,
I see a fiercer flag unrolled
Eclipsing now the red and gold
Infanta of the evening skies.
For now all other flags turn black
Save there, against the stormy rack,
Three crosses in a single wheel—
The spectrum of the light they lack,
And rainbow of the showers of steel!

But this no miracle-crusade
Won in our hearts before we strike;
Rather a punishment-parade
For friend and enemy alike;
Yet when the mealy mouths are heard
Of those who prostitute the word
And in the rearguard pimp for hire,
It's time to imitate the bird
Who preens his chevrons under fire!

To hear the Fire-bird change his score
And match his war-whoop to the drum
As scarce in twenty years before—
"Big Medicine" it was for some

Who with the hoopoe scoop the news
That is not printed in reviews—
The kind they stoned the prophets for,
And lumbering progress never views
Except to boycott or ignore.

This Bird be my heraldic crest
Because his prophecies are banned:
He chucks a regimental chest
And flits across the burning sand
To share those gifts of high bestowal
That seraphim bequeathed our sires
One winter night broadcasting "Noel!"
(Strange news for Isidore and Joel)
To cattlemen by wayside fires.

Was that reported in "The Prattler"
Or "The New Yes-man" of those times,
Or like a diamond-headed rattler
Suppressed, along with Herod's crimes,
While he monopolised the Glaxo
And sopped his bib with granny's tears—
Though in a record flood for years
The baby-killing he attacks so
Had soaked him crimson to the ears!

To cock the wind this flame-red feather,
In my sombrero, be the sign
Prophetic of the coming weather
With no false hankering to 'fine',
And the diploma of a knowledge
So far beyond the scope of college
That whatsoever catch we croon,
Ages and continents, to acknowledge,
In blood or lava scrawl the rune.

★

A Letter from the San Mateo Front

Against the Bogus prophets of the Day
Chained to Corruption, Failure, and Decay,
What can I do but take the trampled sand,
Diestro by the Rightness of my hand,
Whose opening Palm, of Victory the Sign,
Branched from the mesa with the Bread and Wine,
By the same toil engendered as the grain
With many a million more, the Might of Spain,
With palms of triumph foresting the day
To wave the golden harvest on its way,
Of which strong millions, strictly contraband,
I introduce this sample to a Land
Where all the sweet emoluments are thrown
To that snug, sinister, and bungling drone,
The fist-shut Left, so dextrous with the dirk,
The striker, less in battle than from work:
The weed of Life that grows where air is hot
With "Meetings" for its aspidistra-plot:
That leaves its labour to the hammering tongue
And grows, a cactus, out of hot-house dung:
A manual head-ache, fastened in a fist,
And fed with fumes of foul carbonic mist:
A vegetable cramp: a bolted clam
Whose grudging doors on life and daylight slam:
The "No"-to-life translated as "I Am,"
A Life-constricting tetanus of fingers
Under whose sign an outworn Age malingers,
While from its back the nails eat slowly through,
For communists out-fakir the Hindu,
And hanker for stagnation thrice as vast
Where all must starve beneath the lowest Caste:
The fungus that, by still decaying, grows;
Sleep's Aegis, save when dealing dirty blows;
Like the raised claw-bunch of an ancient stork,
With cork-screwed fingers, as a crumpled fork,
In a rheumatic ecstasy of hate
Clenched at the world, for being born too late;

This weary fist infests the world entire
As common in the palace as the byre,
As limply fungoid in the idle rich
As when it grimly toadstools from a ditch,
Or, friend to every cause that rots or fails,[1]
Presides in Bloomsbury with tinted nails;
As doomed anachronisms, Sire and Son,
Capitalist and communist make one,
The scrawny offspring and the bloated sire
Sentenced by nature to the same hot fire;
So in red Bloomsbury the two are tied
Like gangsters to be taken for a ride—
Smug rebels to Society, the tame
Charaders in a dreary parlour game,
Where breaking crockery gives a lawless thrill
And Buffaloes each smug suburban Bill,
Where the Left Fist will pelt you from the fence,
But when you lift a hand in self-defence,
Although it scorns the bourgeois law and state,
Off to the lawyers takes the broken pate,
And at the first sign of a lifted quirt
Will cling his Mother Grundy by the skirt.
From every communist you can unsheath
The snug fat "bourgeois" creeping underneath,
And every Babbit is a foxes' hole
From which a scrawny "comrade" snarls for dole!
So in Red Spain they're fighting side by side
By common desperation both allied,
Both indispensable and no more strange
Than the unhealthy hide is to the mange—
But on our side such itches cannot grow
Since, with us, the whole Donkey had to go!
For though with lies your hearing they belabour
Theirs is the Capital as ours the Labour—
As fat Prieto boasted with a grin
"The Rights are penniless, and cannot win."[2]

[1] "All we have succeeded in producing is totalitarian State Capitalism instead of Communism." Lenin.

[2] Minister of Defence, Indalecio Prieto. "We have by far the greater half of the fleet, all the industrial areas, and superior armaments. But

But nature's elements, except for gold,
Will shun the Communist's convulsive hold,
And it's an axiom that mere eyesight yields—
Grass hates to grow on communistic fields!
The plains and valleys fought upon our side
And rivers to our Victory were allied
That (loosed to whelm us and to flood the land)
Were parted like Red Seas on either hand:
Our comrades' blood, still conscious in their veins,
Headed the waves away with curling manes,[1]
And, swerving on both sides to let us free,
Galloped them foaming headlong to the sea—
In death still present, hand upon the reins,
Such friendship links us riders of the plains.
Nor can a clenched left fist create or fight
With the calm patience of the open Right,
Nor help a needy comrade, as we see
Each time they leave their wounded, when they flee,
When to remove their numbers to the rear
Might sow the grey, demoralizing fear.
Yet see this smuggled Right hand that I bring
The lightest feather moulted from the wing
Of our great Victory, spread from star to star,
With thunder-hackled mountains in her car,
Which all the way from Portugal to France
She inspans in her thundering advance,
Changing their fiery teams at every stage,
For new ones filled with ever-towering rage,
And loosing these in turn to drink and graze
The peace-calm waters and the flowery ways,
Till, last and most superb, the Pyrenees,
Snorting a fiery steam around their knees,
Shall trail her spoor of villages set free
Through waving cornfields to the Midland Sea.

what is even more to our advantage, the rebels are penniless and we have
Napoleon's three requisites for victory, 'Money, money, and more
money.' " The Russians took this money, the property of the Spanish
people, and the biggest gold deposit in the world; and Russia became
second gold-exporter in the world market.

[1] The Reds opened the dam of the Alberche river which flooded the
Tagus valley.

By this light hand, this feather of her wing,
Had you but cared to watch the careless thing—
Just by the mere direction it was blown
This war was long predicted and foreshown—
Directness, Rightness, has that airy power,
Anticipating victory to the hour:
While Leftness fails in all, as it befell
When Strachey prophesied at Teruel.
Through its brown palm as through the map of Spain
The Lucky line runs free of worldly gain
Like Tagus through the brown Castilian plain;
Inept the gadgets of the Mode to peddle,
But while a working stirrup is my treadle,
A serviceable implement enough
To rope a Calf or Red-Neck[1] by the scruff
And treat them kindly though they cut up rough;
Whose knot of nerves, by common labour spliced,
The rope and rein for manicure sufficed,
It scorns the scarlet nail-dye of the Left
And only in dexterity is deft,
Too business-like, unladylike a fist
To tantalize a British Communist,
As found the Tomboys of the Summer Schools
At San Mateo rounded up like mules,
As if they came not here to fight and kill
But to some nudist camp of Swedish drill
With sempahores no soldier understands
First clenching fists then throwing up their hands,
And when they're wearied of their jamboree,
Ask to be bathed and taken home to Tea!

But firstly, to fulfil the boastful promise,
In my last Book, of SAYING IT WITH POMMIES,[2]
To show I was in earnest when I spoke
And did not Dedicate them as a joke,

---

[1] Rooinek, S. African for Limey, Pommie, Rubio, etc.

[2] See dedication of Satirical Poems in "Collected Poems." The Author foresaw the British International Brigade and its surrender at San Mateo, long before the Spanish War, in a vision: and he actually dedicated his prisoners to his wife in a poem printed before the war! Prince Rospigliosi, now a British subject, can witness to this scene.

And though I could not say just where or when
Was certain they would flounder to my pen
Which never yet in prophecy has failed
And had them counted years before they sailed
And over lands and seas were puffed and floated
To within half a mile of where I wrote it—
Equestrian Muse of our Castilian trails,
Accept this offering (as of votive quails)
Of these three hundred Red-Necks, thrilled and caught
By Prophecy, on the live wires of thought,
Brought here to learn why communists "feel small"[1]
And we so perpendicular and tall
(Like a Cathedral over Comrades' Hall)
For whom I sent the gay whip-cracking words
To round them up in flabbergasted herds,
And stretched the wire of rhyme, and switched the shock
That numbed the birdsclaws of their noisy flock—
Those scrawny fists, late screwed into a knot,
But now their manual tetanus forgot,
As with the grapenuts reddening in their crops,
In Roman fashion, they salute the Wops—
Renouncing all their "Meeting"-gotten valiance,
To crawl before a handful of Italians![2]
Whose plight, eloctrocuted half by fear,
Must be my mandate to their Country's Ear—
That huge spittoon of webbed and scarlet gristle,
Credulity's Lofoden, the Niagara
Of Suction, where the lies like whirlwinds whistle,
And to uphold whose weight, a drunken staggerer
Revolving to its windmill-like career,
The Nation groans, the Atlas of its Ear!
And well might Lenin shout, such lugs to spy,
"Well-used, our Mightiest Weapon is the Lie":
With Kosher-cooked Alcazars to be blasted
As badly as the real one was devasted,

[1] Day Lewis, the Rearguard poet, who "fee-foh-fummed" so fero-
ciously in peacetime and then spent the war in an armchair wrote this
line: "Why, when I meet a Communist, do I feel small?"

[2] They were far too scared to surrender to the Spaniards who sent
me over to interpret: they knew what they had asked for! They said
they wished to surrender *en bloc*, to the Italians, but would otherwise
"have to fight" as they knew what they deserved from the Spanish!

Its huge defenceless target weakly wags
And streams in tatters like a hundred flags
For all to spit in—journalists or "highbrows"
(If guaranteed no brain behind the eyebrows)
For Defrocked Scoutmasters and wheedling Jews
The dumb receptacle of doctored news,
Of prophecies so stubbornly perverse
That they work out inspired—in the reverse,
(Like Lockhart's Prague and Strachey's Teruel
No sooner to be published than they fell)
And all those plans that democrats expound
To boomerang, in life, the wrong way round.
Where wowsers may discharge their wondrous lore
Who'll "fight for peace," and yet disarm for war—
This Ear, Public Convenience number One,
For all who rave or froth beneath the Sun,
Which sucks in all that's said, or thought, or written,
And loves by Hebrews to be mauled or bitten,
Yet when I near it, gives a threatening wag,
"For MEMBERS ONLY" running up the flag,
Because I've got the future in my bag
And by the tail can swing that howling cat about,
Who live the things they only chew the fat about,
Since my existence has been lived and fought
As theirs at Oxford ready-made was bought
And in my teens I'd shed like threadbare trousers
Every experience possible to Wowsers;
I know what wrings their withers night and morn
To wish (quite rightly) they had not been born
Since of the English poets on your shelf
The only sort of "Worker" is myself,[1]
Grown wiser in the company of mules
Than they with learned pedantries of fools,

[1] At the time of the great popular National Uprising in Spain, I was
the only foreign writer to be properly affiliated to a union of skilled
workers—the 'Union de Vaqueros'—in Spain and I rose with my comrades, the agricultural workers, that is the lowest-paid and hardest-
working *majority*, against the highly paid minority of miners and factory-
workers, whose work is done for them by machines. It was from the agricultural peasants that Lenin and Stalin got the greatest opposition in Russia.

And, since I was not sent with foreign cash,
Like some, to spread the bolshevistic rash,
Able both to explain the "Spanish Worker"
From the inside, as to expound the Shirker,
The Communist, whose bungling Left we fight
With this Right hand—in every sense the Right!
So that when I approach that Red Left Lug
And honourably would discharge my plug
Of truth, the buckshot of my deadly mug,
To pepper with reality its dream—
Like an anemone, with folding seam,
Into its neck it tries to disappear,
And where it wagged the Man, he wags the ear,—
Who every time contrives to swing the lead
When I would raise my trumpet to his head,
Though in this cud of victory that I chew
There's balsam for the spittle of the Jew:
Since in a land where everything's called New
That's ready to dilapidate in two—
With "New Verse" and "New Statesman" to be new with
Alas, it's a New Newness they could do with!
All things that date the most, this label means,
To-day's boneshakers, last night's crinolines,
That with the latest fashion and the mode
Still to the scrap-heap point the shortest road—
So I must strive its meaning to re-New,
And stir the fossils in their rancid stew,
By showing them a thing they've seldom seen—
A writer who is not a dead machine
Turned out like Ford cars in a time of crisis
From Charlie-factories of Cam or Isis[1]
And only guaranteed to run down-hill
Where failure can be headed for a spill.
For naught have they espoused in prose or rhyme
But perished through incompetence or crime:
What they uphold of its own self will fall
And out the Blums and Beneshes will crawl;
Though Lenin triumphed, into fullness blowing,

[1] Charlie Chaplin, the clown, with his outsize feet, stands to the author as the symbol of *pedestrian* commercial civilization.

Ere these lugubrious Mascots could get going,
That was his luck, for Luck where they appear,
As from a Bunyip,[1] howling flies in fear—
And now poor Lenin's cherished dream of Spain,
Through their support, has gurgled down the drain.
When from his eminence Azaña fell,
It was upon the day they wished him well;
A letter came, from Woolfs and Huxleys sent
Support and sympathy to represent,
And straightway all his energies expired,
Something collapsed in him, he went all tired
And from the State executive was fired:
And flawlessly this axiom has been kept
What Auden chants by Spender shall be wept—
Go, ask the poor old Negus if I lie,
And Largo Caballero, by and by!
For they've signposts that always point the path
First to Geneva, afterwards to Bath,
When, crunched by the Right-handedness they lack,
Each Thug or slaver takes the scrap-yard track,
With these funereal croakers at his back;
Vultures and crows so rally to the field
And where they "group" you know the doom is sealed,
Before it hits our nostrils ripe and hot
They've long ago divined the inward rot,
And as by sympathy I sense the rose
Of Victory before its buds unclose,
So they (before it trumpets to the nose)
Anticipate the maggot on its way,
With it co-operate in swift decay,
And so with one more carcass strew the way:
Which you may spoor, by no exception crossed—
One trail of causes villainously lost!
See, how they come "Democracy" to save
The moment it begins to dig its grave,
While jutting bonework corrugates the scurf,
With murderous paws to shovel its own turf
A starved hyena at whose sapless dugs

[1] Australasian Bogey-Man, which, from all accounts of it, must be
rather terrifying.

The Russian Romulus in frenzy tugs,
While Spanish Remus has the brighter wheeze
To polish off its last remaining fleas—
Till even such a chump as Herbert Read
Woke up to it that things had gone to seed,
And chose the next most mouldy thing he could
That promised nits and jiggers in the wood,
Who now in Anarchism's foetid cell
The elixir of life pretends to smell.
Decrepitude for them's the only Right,
Though as "humanitarians" they write
With greasy Tartuffades to slime the cause
That has more victims in its murderous jaws
Than ever were destroyed in mortal fight,
Blasted with bombs, or heaved with dynamite,
Or executed here, to serve them right:
Not only that, but if we well examine,
Invariably they side with filth and famine,
Morality for them has never mattered,
Except when crime or failure must be flattered:
For all their talk of what is Right or Wrong,
What matters most to them is—"Does it Pong?"
For they'll have nothing but what's stale or late
And to be "modern" must be out of date.
They bury facts as crocodiles their meat
Returning later to "debunk" the treat
Which most they live for; like their friends, the Reds
Who pulled the mouldering corpses from their beds,
Who in Huesca's graveyard raised a Bar,
And drummed with thighbones to the shrill guitar,
Doomed by the same sub-realistic curse
In living bodies to forestall their hearse,
A doomed and dying species, with their cause
Condemned by the inexorable laws,
Who only by inversion can exist
As perverts, in a charnel-breathing mist,
From Death and Sin their scrawny themes to twist—
And with such bards to trumpet them to battle
No wonder British Reds stampede like cattle!
Their "Progress" is to shunt along a track

46

Where "Left" means left-behind and "Front" means back
When was a Front so definitely split
As this fat Rump they have mistook for it,
And shown us little else as we advance
Our proper *Front* from Portugal to France:
And if they're facing "Front"-wards, I'll not quiz
What must the tail be like, if that's the phyz?
With them, for opposites we have to hunt—
"Backward"'s the word, when Popular the "Front."
From Seville to Toledo, every day,
They write up their advances all the way:
With victories they fill their daily sheet,
Woe to our cause, then, if they should retreat—
God save us from their ultimate defeat!
In a whole year when they would do or die
Their sole Alcazar still has been the LIE,
There all their foes are routed, only there
Pusillanimity can fight with prayer!
Put France and England's might upon the main,
The Gold of Moscow, and the loot of Spain,
Have all your mobs from arsenals prepared
Against a cause already thrice despaired,
A country prostrate, so that Moscow's powers,
Can say "Within a fortnight Spain is ours"—
Add but their vows—and all is ineffectual
Once smiled on by the British Intellectual:
For they have spat on Life, the valiant Friend,
Who must be our companion to the end,
And he, no Red-Neck to forgive such fun,
From where they look, will turn away the Sun!
This, which I only whisper to my gun,
To the dry grass, and to a broken tree,
Long after may be heard beyond the sea
When nations catch their ancient health again
From the new might of Resurrected Spain,
That like a miracle, from nothing born,
To nightmare-ridden Europe shows the Morn
And stands between her and the living Hell
No liberal Democracy could quell—
But let these prisoners speak for my precision

And answer for my range and drive of Vision,
Who promised this before the war begun,
And drilled them with my pen before my gun
To dance in dudgeon what I wrote in fun:
And come like "Calais Burghers," as I planned,
"With their pink halters tamely brought to hand"[1]
In every detail fleshed, as fancied then,
When first the Sword was fathered by the Pen:
Surrendering without a single blow
For nothing, save that I foretold it so—
To make this great round-up at San Mateo
A film of my original rodeo—
To see them act down to its quaintest antic
The verse they dared to dream of as "Romantic,"
When (ere they dreamed of it) I had portrayed
The British International Brigade,
And twice predicted clearly in advance
Lest any fool should foist it on to chance
If only once I'd whirled the whistling line
To get them hog-tied with iambic twine,
Preventing all suggestions of coincidence
When the live words should burgeon into incidents,
As in a tame hypnotic trance they follow
My verse, the flaming lariat of Apollo.
See now, like filings to its powerful magnet,
Like barbels gasping in its mighty drag-net,
Daring all likelihood of place or time
To prove my sure trajectory in rhyme,
Trampling geography, deriding space,
To fetch these grapenut-crunchers face to face,
I haul them out of their sub-human trance
Before a true reality to dance.
For the first time by a creative thought

[1] The Pink halter, the ringworm of sunburn, with which the God of
poets and herdsmen, Apollo, brands the necks of Britishers. The Author
had never been to San Mateo yet he saw in a vision the whole scene and
dedicated the British prisoners which he later took there to his wife
in a hermetic poem which was printed and published two years before
the event (p. 111, "Mithraic Emblems"). This is a perfect description
of what happened and couldn't have been bettered had I written it
retrospectively.

Their Joadified existence has been caught,
Their miserable can-can they rehearse
As margin illustrations to my verse,
Projected by its force, gambol by gambol,
Through its side-splitting rigmarole to scramble,
And learn the difference if they didn't know it
Between a left-wing pedant and a poet!
Some fools may find Romantics in my Obra—
But where's a Realism that is sob'rer
When heroes Rooperted in Spauden's line
As dying stoics, nonchalant and fine,
Like numbed, frostbitten bullfrogs to a Cobra,
Galvanically volted through the spine,
Confront the cold Reality of mine?
I warned John Bull to fatten up his son[1]
And Jackie Veal-Calf to be underdone
When with their stainless cutlery and steel
Like waiters they would serve their own cold veal,[2]
Yes, even blobbed with mustard-coloured hair,
Which I'd forgot to order—all was there
A prophet's feast of laughter to prepare!
And vain were all their boycotts to deflect
My prophecies that hiss their hair erect,
Who guaranteed their Popular Behinds
To show a pair of cheeks to all the winds,
And could as easily, in my Delphic rapture,
Have prophesied their slaughter as their capture,
But here the very Quarter-masters vex
For Turkey-food to redden up their necks
Till, all unhurt, we ship them to their shops
With grapenuts still distended in their crops
If we can find any—treating them kindly
To send them home from where they rushed so blindly

[1] "John Bull, go fatten up your son—against my passing by And Jackie Calf be underdone—whether you roast or fry!" So certain was the author before the war that his vision would come true that he not only described the surrender as it afterwards happened but issued prophetic orders to John Bull to send out his sons to be captured: and was on the spot at the rendezvous three years after publication.

[2] See "Mithraic Emblems", "John Bull, go fatten up your son." 1934.

To fling their scraping curtseys to the Wops,
After they'd sacked the Churches, looted farms,
And raised us angry cattlemen in arms—
Leftness of Hand (the shame of work and war)
Disgracing England on a foreign shore,
Whose honour here I battle to restore
From such unholy ridicule to save her.
And when I Bolshevize for Royal Favour
Amongst her Modern Southeys, henna-tressed,
By watering down the Vodka like the rest,
May my Right hand lose cunning, flinch, and waver,
Salaaming there for baksheesh with their best,
Who'll call you honest, daring, fearless, bold,
For blacking boots and doing what you're told,
If only you upclench that "no" to life
And wish your Father hadn't took a wife,
If only you renounce all Faith and Vision
Foresentencing your manhood to derision.
For King's Gold Medals when I strive to please
Their winning will require a sterner test,
No defrocked Scoutmaster could Tupper these
That jingle with the Cross upon my chest:
When Britain and her poets stand for causes
That aren't foredoomed by foul subhuman crime
They'll change their present sanctions to applauses
And own me for the prophet of my time,
Since the whole trouble with the other chaps is
Whatever cause they flunkey for collapses
However well it flourished at the time:
For I foretold La Mancha's Knight would prance
With Charlie like a cockroach on his lance
Which I was called Romantic to believe:
Around the Fates to play at pitch and toss
Like kittens with the skein of Atropos
My devil-daring prophecies had leave;
So happy were the Fates at last to weave
A prophecy that wasn't pusillanimous,
And when they saw my program, were unanimous
I'd come a tedious chapter to relieve:
So merry hummed the wheel and clashed the shears

Was never such a miracle for years
Materialists and wowsers to aggrieve:
For when our cause was scarce a handsbreadth grown
And theirs in blood and arson towered alone
And Absolute from Portugal to France,
With flawless certitude I flung defiance
At all our pundits, bards, and men of Science,
Who've always viewed my gasconades askance,
Since well they know, those paladins of failure!
They've backed no cause from Greenland to Australia
But petered out for fear of worse mischance.
For still the "Southern Stranger" of their theme,[1]
My "Southern Gestures Modify" their dream—
And well may they beware: for from her chain
A "Southern Gesture" liberated Spain.[2]
For where they doze in faint Utopian steam
Among their vicious languors and their lilies,
My Hand will pepper them with Southern chillies
Whenever I can spare it from my team,
As these found out, these gutless weary-willies
Who but that I had called this dance of wowsers
Would still be hiking in their sawn-off trousers
Or climbing grapenut-trees in some green lane—
But that I gave the rendezvous in Spain,
And came to greet them, shouting from my mule,
"Woodley! Old Woodley! welcome Home to School!"
One votive goat, had they but spared my kraal
Would have been worth this batch, their kit, and all,
Who had not even the guts to run away
When their Red Paradise behind them lay
And not a single man to bar their way—
Inviting them with all its charms untold,
The New Jerusalem, the Age of Gold,
Where loving "comrades" howl for gory tripes
And pay their services with shots and swipes.
But take them, Muse, since they were in our contract,
Forgiving me the horseplay of this Entre-Acte,

[1] See Auden's Poem.

[2] A literal fact, Franco flew from exile at Teneriffe.

And oh, sweet sister of Right-handed men,
Be ready to direct my willing pen
With the same constant certitude as when
Though years and seas and lands between us lay,
It goaded them my summons to obey:
And as it then Collectivized one Fool
Out of these Tomboys of the Summer School
Grant that it now may move as many minds
As here it chivvied prominent Behinds—
"Popular Fronts"—ahem! I meant to say
For we can euphemize as well as they—
And so collectivize a Wiser Man
Out of the better specimens of this Clan
Till England is unpommified once more
And poets grace her God-forsaken shore.
For just as ably, and with equal vision,
As I forecapture pommies with precision
And with a breath can puff to non-existence
Three years of time, a thousand miles of distance,
I can distinguish Right from Crying Wrong
And that's the theme and purpose of my song.
So sun my couplets with your radiant smiles
And ride with me these long Castilian miles
Your weight upon the croup behind me swinging,
Your Open Palm upon my thorax clinging,
That palm of victory in whose warm hold
To lullaby a wound my heart is singing
Like a red bird within its frond of gold;
While lovely as the lilt of the guitar
The silence of my rifle sounds afar,
Your jet-blue curls and lips like burning chillies,
Your beauty, like the Giantess of lilies,
Respiring fragrance as we ride along,
The one-horse cavalry whose charge is song,
Two voices underneath a single hat,
Two singers on the same bay bronco sat,
Two melodies in love with the same tune,
That runs in gold and silver to the moon.
Now like the rushing Tagus let us sing
How houses from their blasted ruins spring,

For one bombarded town how twenty rise
And float those long-lost colours to the skies:[1]
How kneeling crowds receive our marching hosts
As if we had been dear, departed ghosts:
As if they had forgot that wine is red
And dazzled by the whiteness of our bread.
The loaves and fishes of an "outworn creed"
Suffice the starving multitude to feed,
And that is wrought by the mere faith of Spain
For which the purse-proud nations strove in vain.
Shiploads from Britain, loaded trains from France
Served but the march of hunger to advance,
As Bread to famine, water turned to thirst,
The miracles of Jesus were reversed:
In vain the Gaucho toiled for their relief
On Pampas thundering with tons of beef—
Round up the plains, or trawl the teeming sea
Where the Red Curse is, there will Hunger be!
The cargoes of a myriad trains and boats
Shrunk to a spider's breakfast in their throats.
They gasp to see our half-ton bullocks bleed
Whom wealth of mighty nations failed to feed,
To see the flocks of fat merinos spring
From some poor provinces where Christ is King,
Where loaves are multiplied from scanty grain
And fishes seem deserters from the main.[2]
Now through the Nation as our legions spread

[1] The Republicans ("patriots" as they were called by the liars of
Fleet Street) abolished the Spanish flag—for the Hammer and Sickle,
a ridiculous tricolor with a liver-coloured stripe, and the red and black
"skull and crossbones" of the anarchists. They never had the effrontery
to call themselves "patriots". They shot people for shouting "Viva
España".

[2] Alas! this was true when written in '38. It was only on the collapse
of the Red front that the amazing achievements of the Nationalists
in husbandry were all drained away to feed the starving multitudes who
had suffered Red rule for close on three years, with four years of republican incompetence before that. The Russian dictator of Red Spain then
decamped with the largest gold deposit in Europe (the property of the
Spanish nation) and the present régime was blamed for the poverty of
Spain!!

The richer by the poorer half is fed:
Beside the lewd inscription, where they sprawl,
From loafing idly charcoaled on the wall
Hammer and Sickle to their labour fall.
Storks to the steeples, rollers to the wires
Return, and swallows to the broken spires—
And men to the religion of their Sires!
Over the blood of martyrs scarcely dry
Toledo, there, against the morning sky
Like some great battle-cruiser from the fight
Returned with Victory (terrific sight!).
God's flagship, she, with shattered sides, presents
Her leaning funnels and her gaping rents,
In high salute uplifts her steepled guns,
And far the deep reverberation runs—
Through echoing gorges of the hills it roars
The listening plain receives it and adores
And at her mast the Royal Ensign soars,
Where one ecstatic eagle soars and faints,
And morning like a red and golden banner
Is roaring in the hurricane hosanna
Of the Heroes, and the Martyrs, and the Saints!

★

Dawn on the Sierra of Gredos

While those of us by Tagus stray
Whom careless Valkyries forgot
Or stayed behind with on the spot—
(Your hair the night, your face the day!)
And others ride the Milky Way
Whose hearts with "greater love" were shot—

In what new Tercio, what battalion,
Serves now our recent Alferez,
The Legionary angel, Death,
The rider of the pale grey stallion,
Who paid the godless hordes their tallion,
And made their wrath a waste of breath?

54

The last of four tall shades, he's ridden,
Along the eastward mountain-track,
Their faces in sombreros hidden
Though by their horses they were known—
The riders of the White, the Black,
The Colorado, and his own.

He will return, but not to harm,
Rather to rest us, and relieve.
He will come back, but as on leave
Or visiting some friendly farm—
No more in the thunderclouds to sleeve
The lightning of his strong right arm.

Like young Morato's eagle heart
His own grew wings, and would not stay
When all our best had got the start,
Outstripped the flesh, their service done,
And joined new Tercios in the Sun
To guard the frontiers of the Day.

High on the Gredos near the sky
His iron hand our own we clapped in
Returning earthwards, Life and I,
When on his way we wished him well
Now in the Seraphry to Captain
Promoted for contempt of Hell.

The shades of night began to trickle
Away, like those whom late the Sickle
And Hammer led to shame and loss
By their own emblems laid quiescent—
So deftly Sickled by the Crescent,
So soundly Hammered with the Cross.

There where the Gredos drops so sheer,
Rearing my horse to wave goodbye,
I caught my lifted cattle-spear
Entangled in the dawn-lit sky
As though some canopy to rear
Or streaming oriflamme to fly.

From Africa away to France,
Flag-tethered to so frail a lance,
It tugged and thundered in my hold—
A whole horizon of horizons
Where crimson clouds, like herded bisons,
Migrated over wastes of gold.

Like the tall sloe-stem that towers
To herd the sunsets as they die
Till (once a century) it flowers
And gives them back to later days
From lion-throated blooms ablaze
To roar its fragrance through the sky.

Like that lit stem, my lance outbroke
With clouds of pollen for its smoke
Igniting into tongues of praise,
While birds, the solar Aviation,
Like morning stars at the creation
Exulting magnified the rays.

Range over range around us rolled
With snow-peaks turning green and gold
And crimson. Nearer to the eye
The Guadarramas rose, like surges
Serrated, when the northwind scourges
Their tops, and makes the spindrift fly.

A swift arcade of poplars white,
The steep Alberche swerved from sight
And in the Tagus sought its father,
And now the day itself showed white
Like wingéd Victory poised for flight
Upon the wreck of the Alcazar.[1]

Down where the lyddite and the "nitro"
Had scorched the base of the sierras,
Blossoming almonds, row on white row,
And flowering peaches, row on red row,
Shelved glimmering down by tier and terrace
To the Arenas of San Pedro.

[1] Pronounced Alcathar in close assonance with father.

I felt as one who bears the dais,
At Corpus, when our King's proud way is,
And wondrous light around him waves,
A rose-red nimbus, trawling fire,
It harps each dark street like a lyre
As water harps the walls of caves.

Toledo's streets those fissured kloofs
Appeared: those ranges scanned her walls,
With woods for people on the roofs,
With cliffs for balconies, for shawls,
The flowering orchards in their falls,
Descending from our horses hoofs.

The day, exultant and serene,
In slow procession passed between
Till like a Phoenix, bleeding fire,
Shot through with arrows of desire,
The Monstrance in the sun was seen
To flame with love as Hell with ire—

The sun, with resurrected brow,
Who dies each day, to teach us how,
Who feeds his blaze with deaths of men
Until it shall devour the sky,
And make the abyss one huge round eye
Of wonder to adorn it then.

I know that blaze, though worlds should shatter,
Its afterclothing for the sprite,
The flesh, when it has taken flight.
For light's the absolute of Matter,
And what the light is to the latter,
The Intellect is to the light.

It is the stuff our comrades burn to
Like incense rising from the mire.
It is the source our bodies yearn to
And our crusading hearts aspire,
Out of the dust that they return to
Translated into song and fire.

We gazed into that light primordial
That filled with love the whole vast region
Whereunto death had passed from here:
So comradely, so frank, so cordial—
Like re-enlisting in the Legion
It made the thought of death appear.

Freed from the locustries of Marx,
The plain sent up a myriad larks,
And Life and I, with time to spare,
Rode homeward down the slope abreast,
And hung our rifles up to rest
And yoked the oxen to the share.

★

Later Poems
(1939-1956)

The Clock in Spain

This Clock from England says he came
Where as a God he was revered.
His hours in length were all the same,
And each departed whence it came
The moment its relief appeared.

To a great Firm his line he traces,
Of manufacturers the aces,
And if you don't believe it's true,
The legend written on his face is
"Birmingham 1922".

Squire was the Auden of those days
And Shanks the Spender of our trade;
For there the Clock awards the bays
And tells the prophets when to fade
Or die of one another's praise.

Like a policeman on his beat
The despot ticked with measured tread,
Dictating when to sleep, or eat,
Or drink—for in the darkest street
No Pub could open till he said.

Hours never telescoped in one
Disjointed by the lovers' thrill,
Nor made the night like water run
To strand the flushed and gasping sun,
Dumbfounded, on their window-sill.

Big Ben proclaimed, through mists of grime,
The surly fascism of Time,
And all the small Benitos, then,
Would cuckoo, tinkle, chirp, or chime
Their orders to the race of men.

Some Red Brigader, panic-shod,
Abandoned here, on Spanish sod,
This sacred fetish of his race
He'd fought to substitute for God—
So we took pity on his case:

And placed him on the mantel here,
Where still he ticked with might and main,
Though, like his countrymen, in vain,
With local ways to interfere
And stop the history of Spain.

The Sun would pause to hear a song
And loiter, when he chose to chime,
Which always put him in the wrong:
And folk would dance the whole night long
When he proclaimed it closing time.

His heart was broken by the trains
Which left him panting hours ahead:
And he was liable to sprains,
For on the wall we knocked his brains
Each time he shrilled us out of bed.

Like Bonaparte upon his isle
Confronted by Sir Hudson Lowe,
The Despot lost his haughty style
Recalling with a rueful dial
His pomp and pride of long ago.

But when, athwart an open door,
He smelt the orange-trees in flower,
And heard the headlong Tagus roar,
And saw the white sierras soar,
That moment cost him half an hour.

And when amidst the poplars white
He heard the nightingales unite
To drown the torrent's hoarse furore,
And held his breath from sheer delight—
It lost him fifty minutes more!

About the time of our Fiesta,
When gales from the meseta sweep
To strew the roses fetlock-deep—
He fell into his first siesta,
And now he often has a sleep.

But what served most to change his story
And turn his notions outside in—
This clock so querulous and hoary
Beheld my love, in all her glory,
Clearing for action to the skin:

Her hair that smokes with raven swirl
To tell of banked and hidden fire,
And golden dynamos that whirl
To launch a battleship of pearl
Into the rollers of desire.

He saw her deep dark eyes ignite
Like radium, or the northern light
That through the blackening ether flies,
And to the voltage of delight
In glittering swordplay fall and rise.

Her eyelashes with jet-black sting
Like scorpions curved: and dark as night
The chevrons on her brows that spring
Like feathers in a condor's wing
Arching their splendour in the height:

The ivory, the jet, the coral,
The dainty groove that dints her back
To take the sting from every moral
And make each jealousy or quarrel
The fiercer aphrodisiac.

The lips that burn like crimson chillies:
The valleys where the thyme uncloses:
The haunches like a bounding filly's:
Her breasts like bruised and bouncing roses—
And all the rest a field of lilies!

The room revolving like a wheel,
The romp, the tussle, then the fight,
The croup of galloping delight
Where rapture rides with rowelled heel,
Without a bridle, through the night.

Since then our clock has ceased to rail
Or tick the time, as if he knew
Time cannot change or custom stale
Those roses roaring in the gale
That, as I rode, around me blew.

Today more tractable you'll find him
And less on edge than was his wont.
In sprays of lilac we've enshrined him:
He stops the moment that you wind him,
Then starts up ticking, if you don't.

And now the pastures breathe their spice,
Twinkling with thyme and fresh anemone,
That punctuality's a vice
He swears today—and what a price
To have to pay for world-hegemony!

So silent with his rusty bell,
This ancient veteran of the shelf,
Whom I can neither pawn nor sell,
Reminds me somewhat of myself,
And if you want the reason, well,

Although he may appear to you
To have renounced his race and era,
His steel is British, cold, and blue,
As ever flashed at Waterloo
Or held the line at Talavera.

And if the dreadful hour should chime
For British blood, and steel as grim,
My clock will wake, and tick the time,
And slope his arms and march—and I'm
The one to fall in step with him.

The loud fire-eating propheteers
Will cross the drink in craven fears,
Or worse, like vulture, crow, and kite-hawk,
Engage in money-making fight-talk
And pick the bones of fusiliers.

Coining the opulence of Babbitts,
Out of the cowardice of rabbits
And mealy kisses of Iscariot,
More plutocratic in their habits,
The more they woo the proletariat—

In vain you'll ask of them the hour
When zero has begun to chime,
And that which pushed this idle pen
Will strike it forth in bursts that rhyme,
The trigger-finger on the Bren.

★

One Transport Lost

Where, packed as tight as space can fit them
The soldiers retch, and snore, and stink,
It was no bunch of flowers that hit them
And woke them up, that night, to drink.

Dashing the bulkheads red with slaughter,
In the steep wash that swept the hold,
Men, corpses, kitbags, blood, and water,
Colliding and commingling rolled.

Some clung, like flies, in fear and wonder,
Clutched to the crossbeams, out of reach,
Till sprayed from thence by jets of thunder
That spouted rumbling from the breach.

In this new world of blast and suction,
The bulkhead tilted to a roof;
Friend aided friend—but to destruction,
And valour seemed its own reproof.

Forced by the pent explosive airs
In the huge death-gasp of its shell,
Or sucked, like Jonah, by their prayers
From forth that spiracle of Hell—

The ones that catapulted from it
Saw the whole hull reverse its dome,
Then ram the depths, like some huge comet,
Flood-lit with phosphorus and foam.

The shark and grampus might reprieve,
After their jaunt upon a raft,
The few that got Survivors' Leave
But those who perished would have laughed!

Their fiercest thirst they've quenched and cupped,
And smashed the glass (this life of slaves!);
No hectoring Redcaps interrupt
Their fornication with the waves.

For us, this world of Joad and Julian,
The dithering of abortive schemes;
For them, the infinite, cerulean
Suspension of desires and dreams.

So save your Bait, you Bards and Thinkers!
For us who daren't refuse to chew
Hook, line, and swivel, trace and sinkers,
And rod and all, and like it too!

For them, the wave, the melancholy
Chant of the wind that tells no lies;
The breakers roll their funeral volley
To which the thundering cliff replies.

The black cape-hens in decent crêpe
Will mourn them till the Last Event;
The roaring headlands of the Cape
Are lions on their monument.

★

The Colloquy of the Sphinx and the Soldier

Across the sands and burning flints,
The huge Gibraltar of the Bints[1]
With half a lion for her crupper,
She who defies the worm and weevil,
With sands and seas and stars coaeval,
Sits with eternity at supper;

Where not a shadow camouflages
The waters of the blue mirages
That sprout with sisal for their cress,
Confronting her, a soldier stands,
The flyblown Pharaoh of the sands
Whose pyramid's the Sergeant's Mess.

[1] The side view of the Sphinx is so like Gibraltar that she might be
called the Gibraltar of the female sex. Bints=women.

Conversing in the Esperanto
Of silence, whose majestic canto
The desert from the soul sublimes—
Of what they spoke I give the sense
Translated into mood and tense
But plead a licence for the rhymes.

'Rock-fortress of your sex and gender!
By "desert-ship"[1] and donkey-tender
Elected as the Naval Base,
Where craft of shingly navigation
And caravans from half creation
Seek shelter from the howl of Space—

Can you assimilate the factors
Of planes, and carriers, tanks and tractors
That threaten to subvert your reign,
Or from your fund of myth and story,
Dispute, or parallel, the glory
Of England, at El Alamein?'

'I had the Macedonian snow-man
But yesterday, and then the Roman,
And then the Corsican, to swank:
Put not your faith in such ideals
As march on caterpillar wheels,
Nor your salvation in a tank.

We've also had some mad inventors—
Of Sphinxes, Minotaurs, and Centaurs,
Though, luckily, they worked in stone,
Else I might not stay home at nights
Nor answer for the appetites
For which you mice might have to groan!

But I (my own refrigerator)
Controlled this animal equator,
As peaks—their vegetable tree-line:

[1] The camel is called "the ship of the desert." Donkeys also abound in Egyptian caravans.

And thus withstood the volted shock
And electrolysis of rock
Into the female and the feline.

But you invent without precision,
And set no notional division
Between the tiger and the male.
Your tiger-headpiece lugs you first,
Yet all the rage with which you're curst
Is dominated in my tail.

The light of my millennial reverie
Is in the certitude that every
Sparrow to fall, or flower to fade,
Is tallied in a harder flint
Than time could chip from this old Bint
Though with the lightning for a blade.

Whether a hangrope or a halter,
Or Old School Tie that none can alter,
Or Rosary exceeding price—
Trivial and tragic both combine,
Twisting a thread of Gordian twine,
The lanyard of your life to splice.

Through rusty grooves, a four-by-two,
Your luck till now has pulled you through—
But chance ignores the rules of chess.
The skyte-hawk falls, the swoop of fate,
And swipes your rations off the plate
Between the cook-house and the mess.

Yes, you may laugh! but in an hour,
Gay as the bee to seek the flower,
Across the sands a bullet sings:
Your comrade falls: and from the spot,
Flushed like a sandgrouse by the shot,
An angel whirrs on startled wings.

Go now: tread lightly: mind the wire:
This life's as beautiful as fire
But always fighting at the bit.

Each moment is too deep to ponder
And swifter than the star that, yonder,
Slid from your sight, as soon as lit.'

'Thank you. Goodnight,' the sergeant said,
'You've set thoughts running in my head
Of how all destinies are blent,
Whether, like you, one merely sits
And has the pyramids for teats,
Or, for one's pyramid, a tent!'

★

Monologue

No disillusionment can gravel,
A mercenary volunteer
Who joins an alien force, to travel
And fight, for fifty pounds a year.
A grizzled sergeant of the pommies,
A gaunt centurion of the wogs,
Can fall for no Utopian promise
The Bait of grasping demagogues.
Against the usurers of tears,
Fraternity, and all that dope,
I learned (while wet behind the ears)
The use of Nelson's telescope.
The Left Wing Prophet, Bard, and Seer,
Sleek Babbitts of the Age to Be,
Who farm this carnage from the rear
Have yet to find a fly on me.
I know the love that shears our fleeces,
The love that makes our thinkers fools,
The love of thirty silver pieces—
A soldier's value, or a mule's!
The same for all who trade in doves
And fatten on the world's distress,

The pedlars of fraternal loves,
And creeping Shylocks of the Press.
Against each rearguard propheteer
And Tartuffe from the M.O.I.,
Experience wads my dainty ear,
And through the solemn bluff, my eye,
For bayonet-practice, punching sawdust,
Lets in the glint I love to see—
For where the sacking gapes the broadest
The daylight laughs and winks at me!

I'm fighting for no better world
But for a worse—the blasted pit
Wherein the bones of this were hurled—
And our hegemony of it!
I'm fighting for a funkhole-warren
Of bureaucrats, who've come to stay,
Because I'd rather, than the foreign
Equivalent, it should be they.
We all become the thing we fight
Till differing solely in the palms
And fists that semaphore (to Right
Or Left) their imbecile salaams.
Each of the other, fifty times,
Will plagiarise the stock-in-trade
Of purges, massacres, and crimes,
Before their hatred is allayed.
For I have lived, of three crusades,
The heroism and the pathos,
Seen how the daft illusion fades,
And learned of victory the bathos.
But when the lava has been poured
Through huge ravines of change and loss,
Of all most hated or adored,
One thing remains intact, the Cross!
It is the rifle on one's shoulder
That galls one on the endless march:
It is the backward-rolling boulder
We sisyphise with backs that arch:
It is the axle of our lorry,

This breakdown planet, bogged in mire:
It is the road we stamp and quarry,
As prisoners, on the sands of fire:
It is the iron that brands us men—
Both friend and enemy as one,
The sword of Victory, and then
The Victor's crutch, when all is done!
Field Marshals, Captains, and Lieutenants
And we poor gunfood of the ranks,
Carry it as a curse or penance
Whether with blasphemy or thanks;
Whether rebelliously, or knowing
And prizing it for what it's worth—
All Heaven upon our thews bestowing
The Atlas-burden of the Earth.

Let me be there to share the strain
And with the poorest pull my weight
As in the Catacombs of Spain
When all the world was Red with hate!
I know that all ideals miscarry,
That cowards use the blows we strike,
That liars aim the guns we carry
Screeching their hatred on the Mike.
Yet lest that burden touch the ground
I would be there to lift that prize,
And with the lowest conscript found
That ever 'Freedom' chained with lies,
Rather than feast on poor men's bones
And cheat the worker of his bread
With Judas-kisses, sighs, and groans,
Between the armchair and the bed.
I love the hard and stony track
Where humour flashes from the flint,
And though on crutches crawling back
Trussed like a turkey on a splint—
If you should ask what other joy
Amongst my fellow-slaves I found:
I dare not speak, I am a Goy—
One of the Christian Underground.

From there, whichever way they work us,
Will boomerang the last surprise—
Out of the red sands of the Circus
The great Cathedrals climbed the skies!

★

Heartbreak Camp

(To Major S. C. Mason of the Nigerian Regiment)

Red as the guardroom lamp
The moon inspects the trees:
High over Heartbreak Camp,
Orion stands at ease:

With buttons lit, for Sentry,
He challenges who's there
Acceding all the entry
Whose passport is Despair.

All joys are privates there
Who seldom go on leave
And only sorrows wear
Three chevrons on their sleeve:

But boredom wears three pips,
A fiend of monstrous size,
With curses on his lips
And circles round his eyes.

All round, for league on league
And labouring up the hills,
The clouds are on fatigue,
Collecting damps and chills.

Sir Dysentery Malaria,
A famous brigadier,
Commands the whole sub-area,
And stalking in his rear,

A more ferocious colonel
Lord Tremens (of the Drunks)
To whose commands infernal
We tremble in our bunks.

Here, till the pale aurora
Dismiss the stars from drill,
I dream of my Señora
Behind the guardroom grille.

In the outcry of crickets
And the silence of guitars,
I watch the lonely pickets
And the slow patrol of stars.

Our vineyard and the terrace
By the Tagus, they recall,
With the Rose of the Sierras,
Whom I love the best of all!

My heart was once her campfire
And burned for her alone,
Fed with the thyme and samphire
That azure days had grown.

My thoughts for their safari
Have scarcely taken wings
Through spaces wide and starry
To hear her stroke the strings.

But ere one word be spoken
A fiend my elbow jogs,
The reverie is broken
By the tomtom of the wogs:

And, all illusions killing,
Upon the stillness jars
A far hyaena drilling
His company of stars.

*

Imitation (and Endorsement) of the Famous Sonnet of Bocage which he Wrote on Active Service Out East

Camões, great Camões! though twins in form
Tally the cursed fates that love to plague us,
Exchanging for our vineyards by the Tagus
The Sacrilegious Headland and the Storm:
Though, like yourself, from Chindwin to Zambezi
In wars and fearful penury I wander,
On vain desires my fevered sighs to squander,
And on the thorns of memory sleep uneasy:
Though trampled by the same vindictive doom,
I pray for sudden death to come tomorrow
And know that peace lies only in the tomb:
And though in shame and all precarious shifts
You were my model—mine's the crowning sorrow
To share your luck, but lack your towering gifts.

★

"Wars Bring Good Times for Poets"
(Headline in a Daily Paper)

Lies! Let the Leftwing Muse on carrion prey
To glut her sleek poltroons, the vulture's kin.
My only pickings were a ranker's pay,
With chevrons on my sleeve, and on my skin.

★

The Moon of Short Rations

Sound me the clash of eating-irons—
The wars where grease and gravy mix!
For in the wind I hear the sirens
Of convoys steaming up the Styx,

And here the rising moon enamels
The skulls of donkeys, mules, and camels,
Whose bonework trellises the track
From here to Headquarters and back,
Which vultures indicate by day
Who roost upon the cook-house shack
Too listless to be scared away.

In better lands, for men's relief,
The breeds for butchery are born,
And there the bullfrog booms his grief
Along the riversides of beef
At bullrise of the sacred horn,
The crescent, sickled in a trillion
Reflectors (Argentine, Brazilian,
Or African) through ranching lands,
Across the plains of bovril, bully,
And biltong, where the belt expands
And the warm air comes curled and woolly
With the refrain of bleating fleeces
Or bristly with the grunts of pork—
Moon of ineffable releases,
Clash me the clink of knife and fork!

Sing me of Sleeping-Car safaris
Through townships blown to smithereens:
The Gold-rush to the Manzanares
Of Bishops, Bards, and Picture-queens
With limelight free, and central heating,
Speeches, and healths, and fat men eating,
While children fought for stale sardines
The better to enhance their pity
And appetise the cocktail-snack,
As in the sewers of the city
We groped, and fought, and stumbled back.
Rivers of burgundy were roaring,
Burgundy that was blood of lives—
Poets, at Circe's shrine adoring,
Sound me the clash of forks and knives!

In better lands the green leaves mottle,
And Boreas opens out his throttle
Down speedways chevroned by the storks.
Lit by the red lamp of the bottle,
Flashes the play of knives and forks.
The Autumn comes with blare of snails
By shepherds blown with lungs of leather,
And where each huddled foothill quails
Beneath huge thundergrapes of weather,
The flocks descend to stockyard rails.
Great hides are stretching in the tannery,
The fat wind reeks with roasted beasts:
Gold in the twilight of the granary
Shimmer the nebulae of feasts.
And out of doors, behold, at morn,
The Samson tresses of the corn—
The strength of armies that expands,
And, vast as ocean, seems to spread
A blond Sahara, sown with hands,
Whose waves are blood, whose sands are bread.
There, when September winds were strident,
Amidst the sword-clash of the reeds,
We flew the sunrise on our trident[1]
Above the groundswell of our steeds
That thundered into suds of spray,
Like some of those that Neptune breeds,
To race them, on the windy bay.
To the guitar that thrilled and bounded,
With female torso on one's thigh—
Valhallan healths and songs resounded,
Till morning, when the tun ran dry.

But now—the vigil with the slain!
Now is the Ramadan of lions,
When he who fought for Christ in Spain
Atoning, to remove the blot,
Crusades for Woolworths and for Lyons,
Tom Driberg, and the ghostly train
Whose love will wash away the spot.

[1] Trident carried by the cowboys of the Camargue.

Like shells with which the beach is starry,
Chalking their whiteness down the shore,
I watch the motionless safari
Of transport that will trek no more,
The caravan of bones, that reaches
To fetch the moon through craggy breaches
Along the avenue of dunes,
With sorrow for the white askari
And hunger for his black platoons.
The ether hums with strange reports,
The winds are dithering wild with news:
Through Africa, huge reefs of quartz
Grind, like the gilded teeth of Jews;
The east is conquering the west;
The future has a face to flee;
The vultures on the cookhouse nest
Like Poets on the B.B.C.
Rocked by the fever in his bunk
The flyblown conscript sees with dread
From his decapitated trunk
The moon remove his rolling head
(Salome whom the fiends predestine!)
And wrap it in the picture-paper,
And place it in her silver messtin,
And up the range revolve and caper
A fox-trot which the winds pursue—
He wakes up howling for his mother
Bathed in a cold mercurial dew.
The strandwolfs call to one another:
Surely some rations must be due!
Give me deep dreams, and may I waken
To the artillery of corks:
And down the mountain sides of bacon,
From thunderclouds of steam, be shaken
Lightnings of cutlery and forks!

★

75

Jungle Eclogue

PERSONAE: Two British N.C.O.'s. The Nat.

1ST N.C.O. It seems we've lost the way for good.

2ND N.C.O.   But, look!
The hill has calved: and much, that we mistook
For landscape, lives (unless it's my malaria)
And moves, and grows, and profiteers in area.
No random herd of buffalo or buck
Could make the waking eyesight come unstuck,
And from its focus swerve to such a pitch
That bush, mirage, or vision—which is which?

1ST N.C.O. Now multiple, now single—yet I trace,
Through all, the blurred refraction of a face;
But if it has a voice that rumour seems
Far less its own, than of the trees and streams,
The whistling of a trillion leafy tongues
To which the ancient forests heave their lungs.

2ND N.C.O. It scares me stiff. Let's slip into this wood
And do a Spaunday while the going's good.

1ST N.C.O. This is some walking Hangover it seems
Sent to molest us from the land of dreams,
Or one of those old Fogies out of books
That startle heroes with their gruesome looks,
And of their birth and lineage make a song
With genealogies four pages long,
Men-mammoths of the Titan's hulking breed
That late in history have run to seed,
Or shifted off the road-maps and the charts
To cultivate the Californian arts.
So showed the Polypheme to the companions
As here this weird abortion of the banyans:
So Caesar's country, bleeding from his sins,
With towers and castles for her curling-pins,

76

Took shape and met him at the swollen drift
Of Rubicon: so looming in the lift,
Shock-headed Adamastor, from his crag,
Came roaring down with sacrilegious brag
To scare the Lusiads, and (last March) ourselves,
Blaring his foghorn from the rocky shelves,
The day we slithered on the tilting deck
And half the convoy got it in the neck.
And so this Eye-sore to the Sergeants came,
MacCallion and MacNobody by name,
Though unlike others of his huffling race
He hesitates, it seems, to state his case.

2ND N.C.O. I fear some phoney mischief of the Japs
   To hypnotise us into booby-traps.
   I have him covered: shall I fire a burst?

1ST N.C.O. Our orders are—Diplomacy at first.
   Keep on the right side of the locals, aim
   To win their friendship and conserve the same.
   Who knows but this may be some playful Yogi
   Designing on our fears to come the Bogey?
   Elephantiasis, of Man, and beast,
   And spirit—is endemic to the east.
   Some outsize rustic yokel this may be,
   And harmlessly disposed to you and me:
   Some local Rhino-gelder, from his size,
   His odour, and the twinkle in his eyes,
   One who sustains the economic push
   De-lousing elephants from tracts of bush,
   Or some old-fashioned farrier of the thunder
   Who's fallen upon evil times (no wonder!) . . .

THE NAT. Wrong, every time! Your brains are both so slight
   That, even were they made of dynamite,
   They could not shift your forage-caps an inch.
   A Fleet of Bombers would not make me flinch—
   And so God help the first of you who plugs
   My Nat-ship with that squittering hose of slugs!

In me you meet the father of the Nats
But keep the knowledge underneath your hats
Since no one will believe you if you don't,
Or shoot a line according to your wont.
Although my voice seems on the air to you,
And you may think you've televised me too,
And tele-stunk me—since you mention smells
It's all in the derangement of your cells.
Because your ears are singing with quinine
Association falsifies the scene:
You think in terms of Radio, as it hums,
Fooled by squeak and whistle in your drums,
And your disordered fancy does the rest
Conjuring nightmares from your fevered breast:
And so you clothe me in the forms you fear
And in my voice—who knows but that you hear
The fight-talk of some paunchy profiteer,
Who broadcasts, dropping aitches for applause,
And froths 'We workers' from his working jaws,
Champing his red civilian hate to froth
And tearing up his enemies like cloth,
Though in his life he never did a stroke
Save write best-sellers for the wealthy folk.
You now insult me with his voice and tone
And see, in me, the monster he has grown
Since such as he can branch, a gruesome race,
Their octopoid antennae through all space,
Destructive Titans, greedy in the gripe,
Long in the ears, and windy in the pipe,
Drunk with their power, blaspheming as they strut,
And mischievous as monkeys on the rut;
These, through the waves of ether, towering rise
With gods and angels to dispute the skies,
Through waves of ether they can scold the stars
And scare the pale inhabitants of Mars
With toad-like hate puffed up beyond amaze
To rule your destinies and guide your ways,
Class against class, to their eternal loss,
To prime with hate—and all against the Cross;
And while they wolf the income and the cash,

To head your empire to its final crash.
As for 'free speech' for which you're bluffed to fight
It's theirs alone, to throttle as you write.
This is the breed you have entrenched at home
By volunteering (Fools!) to cross the foam.
Class them with Polyphemus, Adamastor,
And other bungling hawkers of disaster,
But I, the silent engineer of fate,
Despise that whole Canaille as out of date.
Such out-size hufflers of the beetling brow,
Beside me, are anachronisms now,
And he of whom you spoke, with Godless brag
Who shivers on the aviating crag
Above the rotary abyss, where three
Conflicting currents churn the polar sea—
Is but a quaint survival, whom you saw
Crunching a whole armada in his jaw.
Though, painted with the carnage of his quarrel
His sands were rubies and his foam were coral:
Though in his depths, sharked by the U-boat's crew,
The Red of British valour stripes the blue
As though to stain it yours, and with your blood
To colonise the whole rebellious flood:
Yes, though three Empires sank to stave his power,
There, where your Flag flutters its moth-like hour
And seems to you the iris of the battle
Amid the showers of hot mitraille, that rattle
From here to Madagascar, rip and roar
From thence away beyond the arctic shore—
Yet for his tens my thousands I can slay
And on the nightwind spirit them away.
My power is greater as my fame is less
And leaves more whisky for the Sergeants' Mess,
More empty chairs to splinter into Crosses,
And less of you to Bullshine for your Bosses.
Go count those wooden crosses in the clearing,
In every glade my trophies reappearing,
And own the silent magic of the trees
More potent than his thunder-hackled seas.
Add, too, the Ogre of the Rising Sun

Who hunts you with an automatic gun—
History, when she judges of us three,
Will hand the testimonials to me.
My life is hypodermic: what you spy,
Projected by delirium, is not I,
Who've but to cool your fever one degree
As now I do, that you may hear and see,
And hand it to me, now you see me clear,
That like a fairy sylphid I appear.

Mine is the blitz of hushed anopheles,
The faint and flimsy squadrons of the breeze,
Dive-bombing armies as they snore at ease:
The red blood lit with patriotic fire
That burns for beauty with a fierce desire—
I turn to watery slime, that British wives
May curse for the remainder of their lives.
What's more majestic underneath the sky,
Than when a British Regiment marches by
With rolling drums, and pipes, and colours spread,
And gravel crunching to the rhythmic tread,
The conscript, with the volunteer beside,
Lifted three inches by contagious pride,
And all by comradeship, with ghostly ply,
So harnessed, that the worst for all would die;
Like a great river with its waves of blood
Rolling together, in whose sacred flood
Three noble streams their red alluvium melt,
The Norman and the German and the Celt,
Each in its virtues over all supreme,
Yet, mixed, the attar of this life they seem;
Each from the other breeding what it lacks
In fiery emulation, seems to tax
The rest of nature to produce an equal—
Yet when I breathe on them, behold the sequel!
With drunken stagger by the road they trail,
Friend helping friend, and all to no avail,
With slavering jaws, and eyeballs glazed with lead,
And rambling speech, like spectres of the dead!
The majesty, the might of manly power

Faints at my touch, and withers like a flower.
No armour can avail you when I strike;
Both innocent and guilty fare alike;
The roses on the Red-Cross Sister's cheek,
That, when she smiles, you have no breath to speak—
I turn to funeral lilies in a week.
Nor can the craven shun me in the rear—
War-correspondents, full of pork and beer,
In their snug tent, while writing their despatch
And lying off their heads at every scratch,
Will feel my chilly twinge, and blench, and quake,
And tell the truth entirely by mistake.

Mine are the suns of slow miasmal pomp;
Peril, without adventure, in the swamp;
The green reef creaming through protracted calms,
Dhows passing through the screen of dusty palms,
The rigmarole of Jambos and Salaams:
The solitude of coast-watches who've died
Of their own company—those hollow-eyed
Anchorites of the bush, through wounds or illness
Thrown out of fighting ranks, to face the stillness
Of jungle days. As when some ageing horse
Between the shafts has run his faithful course,
They sell him to the bullring; there he's torn
By the dread silence with its fearful horn
While fever claps the blinkers on his brain
And buries in his flank the spurs of pain;
He perishes with none to heed his call
Save some few scorpions in the crumbling wall.
Now, for your daft intrusion of my reign
You, too, must suffer penitence and pain,
But, for the fact that you have made me laugh,
I spare your next of kin the telegraph.
Prepare, then, to appreciate my art
As from these sacred precincts you depart.
First in the fleecy silence of the ward,
Where through the night I wave my ghostly sword,
Where the mosquito-nets like dangled spooks
Tower to the roof and curtsey on their hooks—

You will be wrung like linen of your sweat
And incubate the nightmares as you fret,
Till, at the tenth relapse, they'll fire you out
Unfit to soldier, but A.1 to tout.
Thence weak and stumbling, with unsteady hand,
Grope your way home—into a foreign land!—
To find that all you fought for (as you thought)
Has turned into the very thing you fought.
The self-same peoples that your oath defends
Against your foes: as if to make amends,
Now shriek beneath the talons of your friends,
Who trample treaties, cozen, and betray
And slaughter with the same delight as they,
Differing only in the fists or palms
That semaphore their imbecile salaams,
Except that, though it's stifled in the news,
Your friends hunt Christians as your foes the Jews
And seeing that the former are more numerous—
Why, that is what appeals to me as humorous!

1ST N.C.O. Arrest the bastard for despondent talk!

THE NAT. Come do your worst. The truth you cannot baulk:
I am within your blood, and all I've spoken
Is of your guttering morale the token.
And I can shake you worse, yes, clear your eyes
Until you envy those you most despise—
Him of the double seawake, in whose track,
Expelled by fear, by profit ogled back
Both ease and riches follow: him who sold
His country's youth for stolen Spanish gold
And pimping safely in the rear purveyed
Cheap bait for cannon fodder: him who prayed
For war, then farmed it in the M.O.I.,
Bewept poor soldiers that were doomed to die,
And beat the drum in loud heroic din
For a fat income and a scatheless skin:
The grigs and earwigs, safe beneath the boulder,
That you, poor Sisyphuses! stooped to shoulder,
And bending, sprained your backs for evermore.

These are the men for whom you won the war
Theirs is the freedom both of speech and thought
(Freedom to gag your own) for which you fought.
But for the Channel, and for such as you,
They would have been "collaborators", too!
Then see your children head-lugged while you wait
From faith and family by the robot State,
Mass-hypnotised, dinned drunken by the tireless
Mechanic repetition of the wireless . . .

2ND N.C.O. Give it a bone! before we say goodnight.
We all become the Evil that we fight.
And if the coward flourishes in splendour
It is enough not to have sold my gender;
This, here, which in myself I carry now
Is all the liberty life can allow,
The only liberty for which I fought—
To live anonymous, to die unbought.

1ST N.C.O. You've said it right; that walking nightmare flits
Restoring us some vestige of our wits:
And now I see the way. One must be deft
When liberty's attacked from Right and Left.
With my left fist the Nazi though I fight
I've banged the bloody Bolshy with my right,
With his own captured arms, his guns and tanks,
Which first we had to rustle from his ranks.
Between the Jewish Fascism of Russia
And gentile Bolshevism farmed on Prussia,
I see no difference save in their salutes,
Though we may have to utilise what suits,
Use, each, a stick, his rival to attack
And break in splinters on the other's back.
One's faith, together with one's native land,
Beyond all ideologies must stand:
When these are reconciled, as now and here,
A fig for all the Nats that may appear!

★

Talking Bronco

In human history, and rightly so,
The Final Word is with the knockout blow,
Except when, to deride that mortal thud,
Courageous martyrs write it down in blood.
Were whacked malingerers to lay the rule
Of what we learn as history at school,
With 'Ifs' and 'Buts' to crutch their limping style
And maunder through the slow, pedestrian mile,
(And that's the role, on which I pulled the chain,
Our British Intellectuals played in Spain)—
We would learn suicide before our dates
And press precocious pistols to our pates,
For inquests than matriculations apter
Before we'd started on the second chapter.
Else, we prefer the company, in books,
Of smiling victors to disgruntled crooks,
When martyrs can't be found whose brighter crown
Outlasts the greenest laurels of renown.
So thus Spain had the verdict either way
Signed with her blood though she had lost the day,
Since five of her first leaders, that were six,
Rushed forth to seize a bridgehead on the Styx,
On duty killed, or that they scorned to fly
When for their blood was raised the wolfish cry:
A fluid Spain's Red "leaders" never stop
To risk although they've promised "the last drop"
Each time they led their bruisers (from the back)
To show a pair of heels to the attack,
Deserting both their wounded and their dead
For driven dupes, not free men bravely led.
As careful of their pockets as their skin
Except when their own comrades do them in
(As happened to Durruti and to Nin)
They left no redder stain their faith to write
Than what they sweat or piddled in their fright
In drops as yellow as their oaths were red—
And as they've written so shall they be read,

With all who try to stutter their apology
(From Duffduff down to Spaunday's last anthology)
And all who farmed the carnage for good pay
Though from the firing they kept far away.
For see the Pasionaria (with her swag)
Escaping weeks before they struck their flag,
Preceded by a dozen fat poltroons
Each with ten dewlaps frilled in red festoons
To pose for anticlerical cartoons,
And dice for loot, in Mexican saloons.
But when the golden guineas cease to clink
And some new racket heaves the seas of ink,
The truth will out, and cry from shore to shore
When Bloomsbury and Fleet Street are no more.
How stale would seem the Epic race of man
Seen through the blinkers of the Also-Ran!
So History looks the winner in the mouth
Though but a dark outsider from the South,
A Talking Bronco, sharked from ear to ear
With laughter, like a running bandolier,
With teeth, like bullets fastened in their clips,
To chew the thunder and to spit the pips,
Ejecting from the breech, in perfect time,
The shells of metre and the shucks of rhyme,
Yet drive the thoughts with perforating aim
Like tracer-bullets on their threads of flame.
Open my lid, inspect my Steinway grin,
And view the shining ivories within.
With such a gadget Samson quelled his foes
And rained the thundering mitraille of blows,
When he invented, chopping men like straw,
The first machine-gun from a Donkey's Jaw.
And shall I scorn such hardware, though my own,
When facing fiercer odds, and all alone?
As many philistines, plus all the Jews
Who ran the jet-Black Market of the News
When in the greatest racket of the ages
Commercial greed conscripted bards and sages
And every scribbler hired his raddled muse,
For Profit in the Barcelona stews;

While only one with something to express
Dared the Almighty Booktrade and the Press
One whom they could not face for all their sneers
Except, by shamming deaf, to stop their ears,
For from one flash of controversial wit
They panicked (they were so unused to it!)
And held (like Aesop's mice) a loud committee
To ban his name from mention in their city,
Since from his pen (as from his bayonet too
Their heroes did) they scampered out of view—
And hence their vain and impotent taboo.
However that may be, it is a Law—
Let nobody deride the Donkey's jaw,
For when men prove too dumb the Gods will pass
The lowdown through the jawbone of an ass,
Or talking horse (whichever comes along)
Providing that the bone is hard and strong,
With blows, or words, that rankle twice as sore,
To cuff them into decency once more!
By tuning up that mandible of bone
Darius' stallion whinnied him a throne:
Achilles' vocal horse, and Balaam's Mule
Could put the best astrologers to school:
And from a horse's kick superb and strong,
The fountain sprang of prophecy and song.
For what is Pegasus, that mystic force,
But part an aeroplane and part a horse,
And part a grand-piano for recitals
With gut and harpstrings humming in his vitals,
Where Beethoven and Bach with angel choirs
Funambulise upon the strings and wires?
Such is the horse I ride across the sky,
Expert in every sphere, to sing or fly,
Or drive a tailshot in MacSpaunday's eye.
And if I'm talking bullshine as you reckon,
Then go and ask the Billygoat at Brecon
Who broke the record of his I.T.C.
With rifle, tommygun, and L.M.G.?
And on the targets wrote his number, name,
And unit with an autograph of flame?

And why the Talking Bronco in the front
With Recces and Commandos takes the brunt
Though by his age, race, domicile, description,
Exempted from all service or conscription?—
While joint MacSpaunday shuns the very strife
He barked for loudest, when mere words were rife,
When to proclaim his proletarian loyalties
Paid well, was safe, raked in the heavy royalties,
And made the Mealy Mouth and Bulging Purse
The hallmark of Contemporary verse.
Then joint MacSpaunday, with quadruple bun
Commercially collectivised in one,
A Cerberus-Hyena, could not cease
His fierce Belligerence (in times of peace!)
But plagiarised from Blimp, ten years before,
The most ferocious arguments of war.
Yet now the Worker gets it in the Neck
Forked by the scruff upon the Trooper's deck—
Collective Rat's the first to leave the wreck,
To gorge, to fatten, and keep whole his hide,
While others bore the Cross for him and died.
His hydra heads, dispersing in a trice,
Unweave in fear their knot of Gordian Splice
With Woodley overseas his oaths to spurn,
Or, with a double seawake, to return,
When Avarice reconquers fear once more
To waft the Prophet to his native shore,
Only returning when the blitz is over
To bum fat sinecures, and bask in clover:
Or, when Conscription-time is due to jump,
Get posted to some rural Fireman's Pump,
To tend wet cabbages from catching fire
And guard the vicar cycling round the shire,
And advertise the fact on blurb and board
For public recognition and reward:
Or in the Admiralty, licking stamps,
To wear a uniform with golden clamps,
Out of his job some aged clerk to Jew
Who thrice as well as he the work could do—
Which Yesmann praises in his "Emu Series"

(That Woolworthiser of ideas and theories)
As "work of national importance"—(Queries!)
Or at the most, if taken in the trawl,
Serve as a grudging Conscript if at all!
Deserters when devotion was most due,
But for the Channel and the bronco few,
They would have been "Collaborators" too!

Then call me all the Horses that you like!—
You will not find such virtues in a Tyke
That follows beaten armies in the rear
Alternately beset with greed and fear
And brings bad luck to every cause he scabies
Far worse than if he'd bitten it with rabies.
No sooner his anthology came out
Than at the sign Spain had no further doubt:
Red hunted Red in carnage through the land—
And yet he blames us that we lent a hand!
His leash of heads will bark, as he has shown,
For every cause or country save his own.
Fortunate Country! to avert an omen
Worse than the leftwing vulture to the Roman.
For where was he, when England stood alone?
This Bogus Proletarian, the Drone
Who stood beside the Worker (*while it paid*)
Seeks every ruse his Gospel to evade
Appeals to privilege of class and wealth,
To save his pockets and preserve his health,
In ministries, where cowardice makes free,
He settles, like the vulture on the tree,
Snuffling his snout in other people's gore
As first in Spain he learned the trick before
With his ten-guinea throat-lump, gilded tear,
And Fox and Metro bringing up the rear,
Commercialising slaughter, with the Deans,
Press-barons, Earls, Bishops, and Picture-Queens,
Who rushed headlong on Sleeping-car Safaris
And made their Klondyke of the Manzanares.
Where Briddish Intellectuals made their pile
And Book-Clubs flourished in prodigious style,

Survey the wilderness they made of Spain
As rich in Sobstuff as devoid of grain,
As fat with tragedy as lean of meat
And full of Copy as forlorn of wheat—
Since there's no villainy at which they'll rest
To cultivate the sobs that sell the best.
A more ferocious, bloodthirsty poltroon
Has never howled for blood beneath the moon
Than joint MacSpaunday, when his leash of heads
To murder, rape, and arson roared the Reds.
For then he "stamped with emphasis" of tone
For "Energy and Energy alone".
He put the test to cruel, killing steel
And from his verdict there was no appeal!
But when in answer to his Fee-Fo-Fum
As to an urgent S.O.S. I come
With "Death to Killers"—yes, he roared for that!—
And "Energy" enough to knock him flat—
Before we've killed a fourth of what they've killed
Or half his rosy daydreams are fulfilled,
A greedy masochist for kicks and blows
He roars for "Justice", as he feels it close,
And yells the more for it, the more he feels
It sinks into his flanks with rising weals.
All Mealy-Mouthed, he changes now to ruth
And natters of "Disinterested Truth"—
So poor Negrin when he'd destroyed the Church
And even the Devil left him in the lurch,
Turned to the Vatican his dying hope
And wired his sad condolence—for the Pope!
Yet what paid propaganda has to do
With abstract "Truth" I'd rather not pursue—
Mine never was the nostrum-peddling manner
To wheedle you salvation—less a tanner.
And surely such Disinterest is funny
That's always on the side of Ready Money,
Nor further from the sales will swerve its spoor
Than ants from trickled honey on the floor,
With no more split between the heart and pocket
Than if the latter were a neckworn locket,

Always with the main chance to coincide
And never into danger glance aside.
Surely (it does not seem too much to plead)
Disinterestedness may sometimes lead
To other goals than those of fear and greed.
Nor does it always move with the same slouch
As the Full Belly and the Bulging Pouch,
Nor always keep so sleek and whole a skin
As wraps the Brave MacSpaunday snug within.
Sometimes at least its pathways may divide
And even with the Book-Trade may collide.
Sometimes its way from Fleet Street widely deviates
A craggy path, which no smug pub alleviates,
And if it's true it has its own set course
You have to hand it to the talking Horse
He sometimes shows that, when it pays the least,
He'll take the mountain path with winter fleeced,
Or volunteering, share the sand and heat
Without a leftwing carpet to his feet.
So if by your Disinterest you swear
Come, ask yourself MacSpaunday when and where
It ever swerved you by one tiny hair
From the main chance, or took a different route
From that which pure self-interest would suit.
Say to confront you with an angry mob
To get you boycotted, or lose your job,
Or land you here beside the talking Pony
Who can do other things than talk bolony.
Quote to me any phrase you ever uttered
Excepting on the side your bread was buttered,
And cite one single case when you were found
Save where the cash and comfort most abound,
As a fifth-column and a trojan horse
In Leftwing ranks to neutralise the force
Of Socialism; mixing milk and water
With the red vodka of diluvial slaughter.
Was it for such "disinterested truth"
That you to butchers sold your country's youth,
Crazing them, like the Gadarene, to die
And trade their tender bacon for a lie,

While in the rear you fattened and grew cosy
By painting sham Utopias pink and rosy,
For which you'd never risk a scratch yourself,
But only brewed the dope for easy pelf.
In vain might talking broncos counsel "Slow!"
And all the direful consequences show
Exactly as it happened four years after—
It only raised some patronising laughter.
But oh, the consternation on your faces,
The day the Talking Bronco kicked the traces!
And though you'd howled for blood, and fire and arson,
Behold you now, the caterwauling parson,
A punctured Tartuffe, oozing mercy, ruth,
And justice, and "disinterested truth!"
So off you went to call the wowsers' meeting
To ban the talking bronco from competing

The "salted" horse that never need the vet see
Owes his inoculation to the tsetse:
Via the cobra's bite we get the serum,
And, further still, to illustrate my theorem,
Mythologers anticipated science
Applying homeopathy to giants;
The hydra is inherent to the hero:
In Fafnir's blood they douche the Herculero:
Achilles from the Styx his temper took,
With frothy gargle hissing in the brook,
Like a hot sword, whose handle was his heel,
Acquiring thus the properties of steel;
So I, in Lethe ducked a thousand times
By wishful critics, make a float of rhymes,
Deriving buoyancy from leaden spite
And like a pearly nautilus, or light
'Portuguese-man-of-war's' more airy kite,
Go sailing with a six-yard thread of sting—
And woe to him that mixes with the thing!

Free verse and prose are slippers for the dons
Unfit to clang this marching age of bronze:

The true vernacular a thorax throws
And leads the rhyme and metre by the nose;
It takes the gradients at a marching tread
Alert for all the ambushes ahead,
And when it finds some wild romantic dream
Has broken loose, with tousled hair astream,
It's easy to collect it on one's pen
As passing troops collect a wayside hen:
And many a dream poor Spaunday lives to cluck
Has ended thus, upon my bayonet stuck,
All neatly barbecued, with careless art,
To fritter on the campfire of my heart!
So you can back the couplet every time,
With its ten fingers twirling thumbs of rhyme,
To seize and clamp the trailing thoughts they fray
And scatter like tobacco by the way,
And in iambics fold them, nearly set,
As nimble fingers scroll a cigarette,
For memory to case them in his breast
And smoke at leisure, as it suits him best.
For what poor Spaunday never understands—
The couplet is a verbal pair of hands
With a two-handed punch, more clean and deft
Than his one-armed and butterfisted Left.
The stumps and bunions of our modern prose
And of free verse, will never pluck the rose,
Or lace the boot, or prime the hand-grenade
That sinks their pink Utopias in the shade,
Though flung from five years distance, in the dark,
To burst prophetic on the chosen mark.
I litter no parades with cornucopias
Of stale ice-cream, or derelict Utopias,
To lie like last week's picnic, spoil the view—
And leave one so much cleaning up to do!

My verse was nourished by Toledo's sun
In whose clear light Ray, Sword, and Pen are one,
One in her soldier-poets of the past,
And here again united in her last:
The Pen a sword, prophetic in advance,

Deriding probability or chance,
That with unerring skill and biting scorn
Can sack a dud republic ere it's born!
The sword a pen to chronicle its deed
And write in scarlet for the world to read:
And both the lightning's thunder-scribbled ray
To singe the daft illusions of the day.
So dazzlingly from hand to hand they switch,
No Leftwing Bard could tell you which is which:
Ere he can name the lightning, forked or sheet,
It whistles up his foothold from his feet,
And sprawls him headlong with its blinding beams
Amongst the wreck of moneymaking dreams.
Like three prongs of one trident, where one hits
The other two will finish off the bits,
Since all together in one flame unite
To foin, to flash, to thunder, or to write!

The libel law your fortified enclosure
To save you from debunking and exposure,
A hydra-headed monster you oppose
To my clean arms, an omnibus of foes,
Stuffed full to bursting like a cat with kittens
With a strange rout of Briddishers and Yitons,
And Bogus Freestaters, and guys gone Yank
Like some farced Trojan horse, or Bolshy tank
With its red farrow, sniping from its womb
At Christian Outposts: but I spell your doom
For truth will out when Fleet Street is no more
And martyrs' blood will cry from shore to shore.
As now today I'm fighting for the Jew
(Since Poles or Finns subsided out of view
Though once the pretext for this war, it's true)
So I have fought for Christians, and my steel
Is always pointed at the tyrant's heel,
Whether from Right or Left he dares to clout
His Maker's image with a butcher's knout.
For Blacks I've done as much, and risked my life,
As since for Jews or Christians in the strife;
When others jumped the liner for Japan

I stayed and faced the music I began.
Had pity stirred you half as much as greed
We might have had a different tale to heed
When half a million Christians had to bleed,
But these were poor and bribed no lawyer's tongue,
Slaughtered by hand, tortured, and heaped, and flung,
To rot like mongrels on a heap of dung,
While you with Herod, and the cash, forsooth
Must blink away the evidence of truth.
But truth will ride and race you to your end,
Propitious enemy and baleful friend!
And as, by night, propelled with frantic strides
A Lion through his forest kingdom rides
Upon the breaking spine of a giraffe
(While all the echoes hold their sides and laugh)
With claws for spurs, and teeth for bridle-chains,
And torn lianas for the flying reins,
And gallops him, with deep, resounding thud
To pitch him headlong in a pool of blood—
So will my verse propel you to your doom,
And give you to the vultures for a tomb!

★

Auguries

Prepare for days of pallor,
Forget the waste of breath.
The day has died of valour,
The night will freeze to death.

And if tomorrow wake,
Comrades, no foe to bomb you,
All you had left to take
Will then be taken from you.

Your hunger, sold in books,
Will fetch huge dividends
To salary the cooks
Of other people's friends.

Your poverty, no more
Your own, but in their hands
Another sword of war
To desolate the lands—

What of yourselves you've wrested
From the devouring flames,
Commercialised, invested,
And harnessed to their aims.

The selves you had, so brave
To suffer, help, and share,
Their pity will enslave
To ration with fresh air.

Their pale, commercial pity,
Conscripting thought and art,
That sits in hushed committee
To vivisect the heart.

The mealy mouth fraternal,
The opening of a purse
That sucks with greed eternal
The wounds it loves to nurse,

The Sucker (hear him smack it!)
Is hungry. Art and speech
Academise the racket
And laureate the leech.

I see the coming day
With golden gifts embrace
The lads who ran away
Or loitered at the base.

Now are the times when Fear
And Avarice grow fat
And drop a pitying tear
Into the pauper's hat.

What rankers paid in taxes
Will clink upon the bar
Where the Left Wing relaxes
In the Swiss or Bolivar.

But we with solemn faces
May hide a secret joy,
In subterranean places,
The laughter of the Goy,

To catacombs returning
Where faith and kindness hold.
And keep an altar burning
To other gods than Gold.

★

How it Works

Salute the free Utopian State
We fought for. Feed, but do not look.
For each free tuppence-worth of Bait,
They charge a dollar on the Hook!

★

Nyanza Moonrise

Aurora to herself, whose white
Meridian, later, was my noon,
And then the dewed approach of night,
And then the rising of the moon.
That these four women were the same,
Though each was of the former born,
This moon reminds me now, whose flame
Bridges an absence as forlorn

Till, like her prayers, the far-shot rays,
Burnish my rifle, touch my brow,
And rule a pathway for my prow
Between the reefs and rocky bays,
With all Nyanza one round eye
To gaze her glory up the sky.

★

After Rubén Darío

One day an earthquake seemed to pass
I felt, with sudden dread,
As if a Babel made of glass
Were splintering in my head.

With Pascal's travelling abyss
I've toured: with Baudelaire
Have felt the wing of madness hiss
And graze my standing hair.

I know the insect in the ointment,
The weevil in the bread,
The eternal ache of disappointment
To all achievement wed.

I whittled up my pens like sticks
And ribboned them with rhyme:
Like banderillas to transfix
The changing hump of time.

But one must win at any price
And fight, to the last breath,
To be the Conqueror of Vice,
Of Madness, and of Death.

★

On the Architect's Designs for the Escorial

This web of faith was drawn so tautly true
That suns are proud its rectitudes to burnish,
And the sierra for its rule to furnish
Pythagorean empires in the blue.
The lines, though airy gossamer and lace,
Dethroned the peaks with their pre-answered prayer;
For what the stars concede to us of space
And what the clouds abandon of the air
Is all pure architecture. The enraptured
Fabric is pinnacled with soaring notions.
By means of stone (with forests, peaks, and oceans)
Worlds in the web of symmetry are captured.
Stone thews the conquering purpose of the line.
When a proud people has decreed its altars,
The mountains move. Fulfilment rarely falters
That dawned in faith—the faith of this design.
Its consummation can be seen the better
Where the stone wrestles, and the ranges yield,
Surrendering the skies they used to shield
And reaching rocky arms for it to fetter.

★

The Lumber-Chest

This vault of oak, while greener oaks decline,
(If memories were leaves) seems still to thicken,
Darken, and grow. It makes the heart-beat quicken
With perfumes, as with draughts of rich, old wine.
With our lives' plunder loading every shelf,
While death-watches are ticking in the rafters,
It fills the loft with sighs and spectral laughters:
And groans, and creaks, and whispers to itself.
It fumes with memories, like Omar's grave
With ghosts of roses, hoarding in its gloom
Musk-scented lace and fans of ostrich-plume—
The swirl, the spray, the nimbus, and the wave

Of tide-borne lust and beauty. There one meets
Dead fashions—bustles, bodices, and bonnets,
With rolls of bills, loveletters, writs, and sonnets
And golden curls wrapped up in old receipts.
See, here, a sword, a ballet-shoe, a pipe
That once consoled: medals of old campaigns
Dried flowers: a pair of spurs, with curbs and reins:
And here and there some faint daguerrotype
Whose spectre with the chill of death impinges.
Heart-breaking chest! What omens do you know
And long to tell us, that you mumble so
When your grim doors grind open on their hinges?

★

Arion

(*To Mary Campbell*)

Limping amongst the prams and bowlers
I dreamed that I had coursed in vain,
My dhow the stallion of the rollers,
My horse the dolphin of the plain.
But you revive them. You refuse,
When by the fireside I would curl;
And with the ripe age of a Muse
Streamline the freshness of a girl,
To set the old momentum free,
To launch me into song, and be
My boat of roses, steed of fire,
At once the courser and the shallop,
The dolphin on whose surge I gallop,
The tune, the rapture, and the lyre!

★

Rhapsody of the Man in Hospital Blues and the "Hyde Park Lancers"

(To the Memory of R.S.M. Charles Mulvey of Princess Pat's Canadian Light Infantry)

From Notting Hill to Prince's Gate
I'd started breaking-in my stick
And of my new, three-legged gait
Acquired the quaint arithmetic.

No more to canter, trot or trippel,
Where dandies prance along the Row,
I coaxed the strange unwieldy cripple
I had become yet feared to know:

In spite of one so ill-adjusted,
So keenly to the task he warmed,
So eagerly to me he trusted,
So newly had he been deformed,

That though he seemed a drunken lout,
Less of a comrade than a weight,
I had no further choice or doubt
But to accept him as my fate.

(So old Sinbad to ruth was wrought
When, thus accosted for a lift,
A chronic pickaback he caught
From the old scrounger by the Drift.)

Then as I pondered this new trouble
Which he'd confided to my care,
Six others passed us, bending double,
Who seemed our fellowship to share—

For in their style was nothing alien,
Those Hyde-Park Lancers, dressed to stun,
In great cocked hats, with slouch Australian,
Though plume or chinstrap they had none.[1]

[1] The name given by soldiers to the Sanitary Scavengers of London County Council. They used to wear hats slightly resembling those worn by the author's regiment, the King's African Rifles, but without the bunch of feathers and the chinstrap.

Like grim knights-errant on their journey,
Couching their broomsticks tipped with pins,
I watched them joust their dismal tourney
Tentpegging garbage into tins.

Identically armed and hatted,
We prodded grimly as we bent:
No last-man-in has ever batted
With a more desperate intent.

In the same action were our talents
Employed, though in a different stead,
Since I was prodding for my balance
And they were prodding for their bread.

Gone was the thunder of great herds,
Lost was the lilt of marching men,
And void the bandolier of words
That feeds the rifle of my pen.

I listened with my six companions
To the low hum of our environ,
And London's streets, like roaring canyons,
With streams of whisky, blood and iron.

Amongst the leafless trees that froze
The wind struck up with flute and fife
The regimental march of those
Who've fallen out of step with life.

We must be silent when men mutter,
We must keep calm when tempers rise,
And when we're shoved into the gutter
It's we who must apologise.

To have one's Cross laid on inside
Abates no ardour in the strife
Though something in us might have died
Yet something more had come to life.

*

Ballad of Don Juan Tenorio and the Statue of the Comendador

Ten cuckolds, slain without confession
In duels, by the waterfront
Of Hades, in a glum procession
Are singing out for Charon's punt.

Ten weeping women dry their clothes
Washed up along the homeless sands
By the red sea of perjured oaths
That shoals with amputated hands.

These were the fruits of all your swagger!
But through their tears will swim no more
Those ice-cold fish, your sword and dagger,
Whose fin-wake is a streak of gore;

For now the hour is aiming at you,
Tenorio! with its finger hooked:
Remember when you cuffed the statue
Upon the grave: and how it looked:

And how it seemed to nod its head
When you invited it to dine.
If you were wise to tempt the dead
You verify to-night, at nine.

The stars are like cicadas chirping
With cold: but it is snug in here,
The throne of opulence usurping,
Beneath this costly chandelier.

The firelight twinkles on the jewels
Of pistol-butts: the rays enthrall
The glinting cutlery of duels
That hang for trophies round the wall.

Your Rolls sleeps safely in its garage,
Your Derby-winner in his stall:
But with a prayer balloon your barrage
Against the doom that's due to fall.

Pay off your cook and sack your butler:
Renounce your sacrilegious vow:
Though Satan were Toledo's cutler
No swordplay could avail you now.

A sentence Lawyers cannot garble
Has just been read: the tombs are still:
But from their garrisons of marble
One headstone moves along the hill.

The wind begins to grow much colder,
The grass with icicles to clink:
To pedestal the skating boulder
Each rivulet becomes a rink.

The river bridged itself with crystal
To its refrigerating tread.
The moon rose masked, and cocked the pistol
Of silence to the world's bald head.

Its passing starched the breath of bulls
Along the Guadalquivir's shore,
And froze the ferryman who pulls
More at his wineskin than his oar.

It seems your hounds have scented trouble.
The room grows arctic: moments drag:
Tenorio! pour yourself a double
To entertain the stalking crag.

Tenorio! it's too late for banter,
The statue knocks; the door gives way:
The whisky froze in the decanter
And has not melted to this day.

One handshake: then the detonation:
A stench of nitre fills the hall:
The Butler on investigation
Retrieved one tiepin: that was all.

Out to the tombs the Civil Guard
Followed the clues of all they heard.
But though one hand seemed slightly charred,
The statue would not speak one word.

★

Spooring an Angel
(For Dame Commander Edith Sitwell)

The harper who discloses,
Hair-triggered on the sight with strands of fire,
The tiger in the roses
His harp of burning wire,—
And with the nerves of danger strings his lyre:
The archer, by whose science,
The index and the eye as one became,
In rhythmical alliance,
To slay with flawless aim
Or limn the flying forms in hues of flame;
By whom the eagle's feather,
The arrow-tufting plume that steered the dart
Stained, with the barb together,
Red, in the bison's heart,
First brushed the cavern wall with human art;
With him to be their shepherd
The zebras strum the wind with silver bars,
It was his aim that peppered
The velvet of the leopard,
Like midnight, with the buckshot of the stars.
His hunting brought me luck:
A woman by his assegai was struck
And, volted to the marrow
By that supernal arrow,

Fell kicking in the lilies like a buck.
I strain my failing powers
Yet only find the cinders where he camped,
Though by his spoor of flowers
I trail him through the hours—
The roses that his flying steeds have champed.
The fletcher, and the farrier
Who shod the flight of all fleet-footed things,
He shot the hawk and harrier
And swordfish from his slings—
Projectiles of a joy that has no barrier.
A legion of disguises
He captains. He devises, every day,
Miraculous surprises,
And as a bird arises
Where as a fish he vanished into spray.
So feathered, finned, and fanned
All speary strengths were formed to his design—
The sinews of my hand,
The windrows in the sand,
The bonework of the tunny's vaulting spine;
Flames, ripples, ferns and clouds
That speak the selfsame language of surprise,
Where seraphs weave their shrouds,
If only to our eyes,
In fiercer resurrections to arise!
The handwriting's the same,
The style is personal. All solar traffic
Of feathers, fronds, or flame
Indicates his one name
And signature. The ciphers are seraphic.
I seek him, wait his hour,
And contemplate the forms of speed and power,
Till I could almost capture
The trance of frozen rapture
That moors the kestrel by the sailing tower.

★

The Rodeo of the Centaurs

(For David and Poppa Wright)

Where the tired Argonaut last beached his skiff
To vanish with the river nymphs: as if
Our breed had not departed long ago,
I hear a voice, and one that I should know—
Chiron's, I'll swear! wheeling the whole great drove
To muster by the fennel-scented cove:
In answer to whose ancient rallying-cry
I've left my constellation in the sky.
Loud flutes the oriole in the berried ash;
White on white sands the dark-blue wavelets flash;
The great wood-pigeons hurl to left and right
The clattering whinny of their headlong flight
Through milk-white poplar-trees that colonnade
Beside the stream, an aqueduct of shade,
Then, as they near the sea-cliff, slack their stride
Of silver places, falter, and divide,
And let the stream fall sheer, like powdered snow,
Or a white horsetail, through its six-rayed bow,
Till with the kindred whiteness it can mingle
Of sister-foam, and salt, and creaming shingle.

Little has changed, except these girls—to trees,
Whom once we knew by name, the Heliades,
The myriad-flaking snowstorm of whose boughs
Is never still, though the cicadas drowse
And the winds sleep. But now the longed-for sound,
As of rock-rolling torrents underground,
Approaches, makes the hollow earth its drum
And waves the oleanders as they come—
Squadrons on squadrons, cantering abreast,
With cattle-spears and tridents borne at rest,
Tilting huge wineskins from their shoulders slung,
Discoursing in the old equestrian tongue,
Waving sombreros, strumming light guitars,
Or detonating stockwhips to the stars—

The sacred quadrupeds, for whose sake time
First flowered with knowledge, harmony, and rhyme.
Half gods, half brutes; they stem from stud celestial
And coarsest horseflesh too. Divine yet bestial—
Divine as was that madness when their sire
Embraced the cumulus of hail and fire
And dared to fall enamoured of the storm:
And bestial as the huge and prostrate form
It left of him, when, by the lightning shot
And heedless of the race he had begot,
It stretched him on the wheel of such huge girth
Its spokes are ages and its orb the earth.
Wisest of all earth's breeds, they suffer most
Yet laugh and sing the loudest of the host,
Though fiercelier bisected by the line
That separates the monstrous and divine—
Than man or woman, who are forced to tame
Two warring natures in a single frame:
Than fauns or sirens far more strangely tainted:
Even than the minotaur less self-acquainted:
Only the Sphinx is to itself as strange
Whose mind through equal mysteries can range
And knows, as they do, that a God must die
Of love, lest on our heads should fall the sky.
They know of things unnamed in human breath
And why the fairest women smell of death,
Death, and the sea, and Charon's spectral bark,
And pollen from the hushed rose of the dark.
And that in their saliva is the hiss
Of breath indrawn above some vast abyss,
I, Nessus, learned from Dejanira's lips
Whose taste the fatal shaft could not eclipse.

Monstrosity is the awed exclamation
Of universes at their own creation;
Wherever a new world is seen to rise,
The hybrid is its utterance of surprise,
And with the forms of beast or fish or bird
Divine or human lineaments are blurred.

Hosanna, blasphemy, or screech or fright,
In seraph, gorgon, or hermaphrodite,
Answer their maker's overcharge of power;
In beauty, shame, or terror, flame or cower;
Or turn upon their maker in revolt,
Out of his fist to wrest the thunderbolt,
In Titans: but in centaurs, deeply wise,
Eternal wonder finds its shape and size.

Enormous stallions captain their array
White, colorado, piebald, roan, or grey,
Bearded like rivergods, maned like the lion,
The very firstborn children of Ixion;
With (in their hoofbeats thundering aloud)
The lightnings of their old maternal cloud,
Though in their cries sounds, too, the ring of steel
Which tells of the inexorable wheel,
Around them frisk, and caper, and cavort
The youngsters, fettled out for crazy sport,
Beardless, and bronzed, with pillion-tempting shapes,
Apt for a thousand robberies and rapes
Of nymphs, or lusty dames, or maiden lilies,
Or rustling their own mares and sister-fillies
From their own fathers' care: or waging fights
With satyrs rolling boulders down the heights.
But most of all their mares excite your wonder
In whom the lady cleaves the beast asunder
Forked from the hips into a surge of thunder
Like Venus when half-risen from the breaker,
Waist-deep in foam, she felt the tempest take her;
Amidst the cyclone of her own red hair
Burned motionless in the revolving air;
And in its angry vortex found the calm
Of the still taper and the windless palm.
Or as the sacred aloe skyward rears
That flowers but once in every hundred years
Stirs the dead lava through its crust of snow
Reviving fires that long had ceased to glow,
Resolving these in living sap to run
And rise erupting to the noonday sun,

Till, white without, but red within as blood,
To rift the pod with its explosive bud,
Smoking its pollen forth in fumes of gold
As though the fleece of Colchos were unrolled,
The bloom whose yawn is redder than a panther's,
With snarl of fire and slash of golden anthers,
Gashes its great glory from the blue—
So from the brute the goddess burgeons through.
Than these two natures, never day and night
At dawn did more magnificently fight;
Nor the pole sheer away from its equator
To such an arctic blaze; nor from its crater
The snow-coned flame more frostily ignite
Its red-gold tresses trawling through the height.

Hippea there, the boldest of the troop,
Her hand a pistol-shot on her own croup,
Leaping the chasmed stream, romps into sight,
Titupping down the grass with daisies white.
So smoothly to a trot she changed her trippel
That on her breast it scarcely bounced the nipple.
While like a mitrailleuse of silver shots
Her one white stocking flickers as she trots,
She swerved into the forefront of the trek,
Unslung the light guitar from round her neck,
And to its music thrummed herself along:
And there were red carnations in her song
And one, snow-white, behind her ear. Thick shoaled,
Like blood-red mullet in a seine of gold,
The deeper shadows in her chestnut hair.
Freckled like rose-shot apricots, her bare
Shoulders and breasts and neck, beneath whose tan
Blurred veins of jacaranda forked and ran.
She snowed with graces, and her eyes with blue
Electric stars that pitied as they slew.
Like flint to steel her teeth the sunbeams broke
And flashed and sparkled as she smiled or spoke.
Like full red peppers were her laughing lips,
And downward from the snowline of her hips,
Like lava'd slopes, the muscles of the steed

Forth like a mountain-torrent hurled her speed
To swirl, to pause, in reveries to doze,
Or cataract in thunder as she chose.
The sailing horseflesh like a frigate strong
Followed its matchless figurehead along
And daisies sprang beneath her all the way
To spoor her passage with a wake of spray;
Two thousand years of youth as fair as Flora
Since for this noon she dawned, her own aurora;
When from the breaking cloud and broken Titan
Our breed began to thunder and to lighten,
Stampeding forth on hoofs like rolling boulders,
Or the red landslide when Vesuvius smoulders—
Out of the womb of ruin leapt her form
And was the rainbow of that raging storm.
Such beauty can be only born of strife
And men can only wrest it out of life
By sacrifice, in the fore-front of danger,
Where strip the battle-nymphs to greet the stranger
And call their lovers from the ranks of doom;
Or where the sylph of pity fans the gloom
And stripes the carnage with her gorgeous plume.

Fillies as lovely, stallions thrice as strong
Returned that day to join their tribal throng;
They drank, they danced, they chanted ancient rhymes,
And boasted of the old equestrian times.
Here where, of old, the prince of music-makers
Had galloped, rounding up the deep-sea breakers
With music, on a grampus for his steed,
Along the rolling, green, star-clovered mead,
The Centaurs met once more beside the ocean;
And having praised all life and light and motion,
Earth, Sea, and Sky, and their Creator most,
Each one returned to his eternal post
And mounted guard in the imagination,
Taking once more his fixed, heraldic station
In poem, sculpture, frieze, or constellation.
The conches sounded for the tide to flow
And, reddened by the evening afterglow,

With the new moon horned in their silver brows,
The waves, like Herefords, came forth to browse
The deep green darkness by the windless shore
Along whose cliffs those hoofs will sound no more.

★

Félibre
(To Frédéric Mistral, Neveu)

Of all the immortality-concoctors
Who cook their would-be by their midnight lamps—
They blame me that I shun my fellow-doctors
To haunt the quays, the markets, and the camps.

Yeats on his intellect could pull the blinds
Rapping up spooks. He fell for freaks and phoneys.
Weird blue-stockings with damp, flatfooted minds,
Theosophists and fakirs, were his cronies.

I, too, can loose my Pegasus to graze,
Carouse with drunken fiddlers at the Fair,
And with the yokelry on market days
Jingle in spurs and sheepskins round the square.

They say it is a waste of time. I differ.
To learn should be as easy as to look.
You could not pass examinations stiffer,
Nor sweat a deeper learning from the book—

Than to be passed for native by the million
When chiming in at horsefairs with my bid.
This taught me the Gallego and Castilian
By which I know my "Lusiads" and the "Cid".

Comradeship, though it's dated and antique,
Is all the Anthropology I know.
The Zulu and Swahili that I speak
I learned no more than water learned to flow.

Collective writers at my name grow raucous,
And pedants raise a loud indignant cry
Like the New Critics and the Kenyon caucus—
Or poultry, when a falcon cruises by!

I've had my share of solitudes and caverns.
What mountain-tops could teach I learned of old,
But got the true Provençal in the taverns
By which I sailed into the "Isles of Gold".[1]

To sit with Mistral under the green laurels
From which his children gathered me my crown,[2]
While the deep wine that is the end of quarrels
Glows through me like the sunset going down.

★

Nativity

All creatures then rejoiced, save that the Seven
    Capital steers of whom I am a herder
        (My Cloven heart their hoofprint in the mire)
With bloodshot glare interrogated heaven,
        And, back to back, with lowered horns of murder
        From spiracles of fury spirted fire.

Never so joyfully the brave cocks crew—
    No more by turns, but all with one accord.
        Never so early woke the mule and ox
Since it was day before the east was blue:
        Mary was dawn, the Sunrise was our Lord,
            And Joseph was the watchtower on the rocks.

Never for such a golden quilt lay blooming
    The fields, as for this richly-laden hay,
        And though the frost was sharp before the day,
The mule and ox, whose respiration fuming

[1] The title of Mistral's Lyrical Poems, "Lis Isclo d'Or."
[2] The Crown of a "Soci dou Felibrige": awarded to the author at Avignon 1953 by the poets of the Provençal Language.

Ignited in the lantern's dim, red ray,
    Warmed him with rosy feathers where he lay.

Far overhead streamed on the signal meteor,
    The Ariadne of the maps, who slowly
        Unwound the light and reeled the darkness up.
Love filled with fierce delight the humblest creature
    As heaven fills an eye, or as the Holy
        Infinitude the wafer and the cup.

Shepherds and kings and cowboys knelt around
    And marvelled that, while they could feel the power
        Whose rapture roars in God, yet God should moan:
And while His glory raised men off the ground
    (For Eve had brought such jewels in her dower)
        The tears of man should shine in God alone.

★

Fishing Boats in Martigues

Around the quays, kicked off in twos
The Four Winds dry their wooden shoes.

★

To My ex-Schoolmaster, Bill Payn of the D.H.S.

You say you are no poet, but
You're more than one, great Bill!
The whet-stone, though it cannot cut,
Can sharpen swords that will.

★

Autobiography in Fifty Kicks

If you hear of my death, do not worry two hoots.
It will mean that Existence is changing its boots.
For my lot is the football's, in pleasure or strife,
Addicted to getting a kick out of life.
The first kick I had was my grandmother's gift,
The kick of a rifle I scarcely could lift,
When the great Koodoo-bull saw the last of his days
And hunter and quarry were skilled both ways,
The next kick I got from the rod in my hold,
As through the green water the mullet I trolled,
And the shark, like a maid unsuspecting her fate,
Turned up his white belly to swallow the bait—
And a terror to hold was the shrieking bamboo
When the fighting sea-tiger had buckled it to!
The next I received when the plaza was full,
The kick of a lance in the hump of a bull.
But then I got one from a hoof of the Devil
And it took me a couple of years to get level,
When down went his headpiece, and up went his tail,
As the fire-banderillas roared out on the gale!
Then the kick of a bronco that bounced like a ball
And laid me out limp in the mire of the kraal—
And the kick retrospective, the kick, the collective
Accumulate kick one gets out of it all.
For it all totalled up to the kick that is best—
The kick that one gets from enjoying a rest.

Once my scholarship won me a kick in the pants
For proving the pyramids built by white-ants.
And still I am prone to pedantic delights.
I get such a kick from historical sights!
The kick of my heart, like a punch on the rib
To see the "Ark Royal" returning to "Gib"
As that great swan of victory rippled the tide
With a hole in her decks, and a list in her side;
To see the Alcázar, reduced to mere slag,
Disdainfully waving her bullet-torn flag—

And the kick (such as maidens must dream in their beds!)
When over the Tagus we booted the Reds,
With the Crescent for Sickle, for Hammer the Cross,
And the thugs of the Kremlin behowling their loss,
As Herod made off with his smashed titty-bottles
To pass round the hat for the babies he throttles,
And the captured munitions were piled to such height
That it seemed that the mountains had calved overnight.

Now the koodoo and sable may graze on their run
For I've tried all the kicks out of life, except one.
It's a two-booted kick, to whose impact aglow,
Clean over the goal-posts of glory I go,
And never come down, but sail on, like a dove . . .
And it comes from the friends and the books that I love.
The best is my Muse, this companion of mine,
Who has learned, like de Lenclos, to age like good wine,
And the scent of her hair is the wind in the pine.
As black as the future that looms in our way
(I like it that colour, forbode what it may!)
Her hair is my night—but her face is my day.
With the wealth of the Muses my bookshelves are straining,
My trestles, of Bacchus, as shrilly complaining.
And we say to our friends, both the living and dead,
"Be with us tonight while the table is spread."
But though with its lading my wood may be sore,
My leather is game to continue the score—
And I say to my Life "Come and kick me once more!"

★

¡Caramba!

Her firm proud flesh admits no queries,
Clear statement which you cannot garble,
Wherein the bust and rump of Ceres
Roll in the rhetoric of marble.

115

Touch but the trigger of desire
To which her beauty is the Bren
With kisses she will open fire
Far worthier for gods than men.
Her tints are in the rainbow seen.
Red laughters on her lips rejoice.
Orange her hair, her eyes are green,
And ultra-violet is her voice.
I faked all that. Did she exist,
Or were she someone I had known,
I would not care. She'd not be missed.
I have one better, of my own!

★

The Ancient Horse Breaker
(*For my ex-Partner, "Triguito", of Ciudad Rodrigo*)

Incertitude my easy norm,
Thought to Security conform
A Nation whose Collective Denture
Grins ghastly as the Barrier Reef:
Each leaf is my Insurance Form
That whirls before the rising storm.
It is to Hazard and Adventure
I go for Unemployed Relief.

Chased by the Night with lifted truncheon
Ere it could wolf its rancid luncheon,
All zebra-striped with petty scandal,
Each Sunday afternoon would fade:
And while each robot stuffed his tunic
From Food-Forms Roneo'd in Runic,
And at her hurdy-gurdy handle
Britannia ground for Marshal Aid.

With poorer folk I sunned my sores
Till nectar sweated from the pores,
For suffering tops the peaks of mystery
When borne in patience with the brace:

And thereupon its heights terrific,
I glimpsed, like Cortes the Pacific,
The sea to which all earthly history
Is as a raindrop to the wave.

I can say grace for Housman, Hardy,
And all whose thanks were grudged or tardy
That life is not all cakes and ices
When they had gate-crashed Birth-Control,—
Grace for this life its saline savour,
And condiments of fiery flavour—
Toil, hardship, danger—burning spices
And hot, red chillies for the soul!

Rather than mechanised enslavement
I'd crawl a cripple on the pavement
Or die a beggar in the drains
Of Barcelona or Madrid,
With Welfare from the fourth dimension
And Charity for all my pension.
My Sociology contains
No other word, and never did.

To every port I am enticed
Where reigns the poverty of Christ
Or comradeship with hardship dwells—
Where Lisbon from an old red sail
Looms out: or on the sky above,
Discharging thunderbolts of love,
Toledo soars with rolling Bells,
Of all my errantries the Grail!

To test my knowledge, as I come
From Fair to Fair, from slum to slum,
While changeless cities catalyse
Each metamorphosis I am,
My Maker's Image, now my law,
Pythagorises with its awe
Each jungle of electric eyes
To which the tiger is the tram:

Or here divides the roasted ox
At high Penedo of the rocks,
Presiding at our Fair-day meal
Over the clouds and sailing towers,
Where chance designs, above the farms,
My momentary coat of arms—
Five orioles in a catherine wheel
Between the red pomegranate flowers!

★

Counsel

The world is pitiless and lewdly jeers
All tragedy. Anticipate your loss.
Weep silently, in secret. Hide your tears,
So to become accustomed to your cross.

Alone grief can ennoble us. She only
Is grand and pure. Then learn to love her now—
To be your muse, when you are left and lonely,
And lay the last green laurels on your brow.

She will be sent from Heaven. The seraphic
Language she speaks in, you should learn, for she
Can talk no other in your daily traffic

When you receive her to replace your bride.
Pray humbly, too, to God, that she may be
A constant, kind companion at your side.

★

Twin Reflections

Like an Atlantic roller, steep and strong,
She hit me, broke on me, and hid the sun.
I surfed a foam of roses all night long.
Day broke with two auroras. She was one.

White Pegasus, with jet-blue mane astream,
Her girlhood reared and bolted me astray,
The jockey to a thunderbolt of cream
Galloping headlong up the Milky Way.

Stacked thirty-high the zodiacs tiered above us
The trumpet in our blood sang out for strife.
In rushed the Minotaur. It was our Love,
And both of us were fighting then for life.

When from its black toril the rapture volleyed
To toss and gore us, in one shambles thrown—
To such a fall, what triumph is not squalid?
To such a death, what life is worth a groan?

Each enemy of Nature bit the ground,
Insanely bleating like a butchered beast,
For us alone the trumpets seemed to sound
Each time the throes of rapture were released.

Two scorpions curved to sting, their spines one hoop,
We seemed, that in a single death expire:
Two planes colliding as they loop the loop
Each having shot the other into fire.

Tired with our strength, the night of years grew pale,
And into waves of crimson sank the dark
To perish like an ocean-heaving whale
Torpedoed by a swordfish and a shark.

The stars, like kisses, had devoured the night
Of rage and battle, into one huge star.
And suavely into rhythm with its light
We wake at peace, and wonder what we are.

If you have seen an almond-tree in bud
Sprayed on the dawn like Biscay on the piers,
Flushed from within, as if with conscious blood,
Yet glittering with dew, like chandeliers—

Such is her wrestling whiteness, even yet,
Where beauty strives with age, as art with time,
But it was with her eyes, that scorn to set,
She made herself immortal and my rhyme.

In their dark fire I saw myself made younger
Star-twinned, with Castor, in the night to shine.
Far into their huge depths, with mystic hunger,
Two breathless Muses gazed at her from mine.

★

To M. C.

Of what these whirlwind times prepare
Perception should be frontal,
These days when Might is Right
And Evil is the drill.

The myriad beast, its rage despair,
Whose might is mastodontal,
The more it wins in fight
Wallows more basely still.

The choice is slavery or prayer,
The bloody course or fontal,
When envy, fraud, and spite
Whirl, and destroy, and kill.

Our joy be in the centre there
Where death is horizontal,
Where faith stands bolt upright
And cyclones keep you still.

November Nights

On the westmost point of Europe, where it blows with might and
  main,
While loudly on the village-spires the weathercocks are shrieking,
And gusty showers, like kettledrums, are rattled on the pane,
The rafters like the shrouds of some old sailing-ship are creaking,
And the building reels and rumbles as it rides the wind and rain.

The treetops clash their antlers in their ultimate dishevelry:
The combers crash along the cliffs to swell the dreadful revelry,
And to the nightlong blaring of the lighthouse on the rocks
The fog-horns of the ships reply. The wolves in all their devilry,
Starved out of the sierras, have been slaughtering the flocks.

Now peasants shun the muddy fields, and fisherfolk the shores.
It is the time the weather finds the wounds of bygone wars,
And never to a charger did I take as I have done
To cantering the rocking-chair, my Pegasus, indoors,
For my olives have been gathered and my grapes are in the tun.

Between the gusts the wolves raise up a long-drawn howl of woe:
The mastiff whines, with bristled hair, beside us cowering low,
But for the firelight on your face I would not change the sun,
Nor would I change a moment of our winter-season, no,
For our springtime with its orioles and roses long ago.

★

Papyrus
(To John and Audrey Sutherland)

Tragelaph and hippotragus
(While I graded as the Magus
Of their hieroglyphic spoors)
Were the printers of my journal
Dinted in the dews diurnal
On the silver-sanded shores,

Where, with summer floods inflated,
Blue Zambesi rolls elated
With the glory of her creatures,
Ornithologizing mud
Into flames as red as blood,
And papyrus into meteors.

There the noonday sky is star-lit
With a galaxy in scarlet
Should a shot ring down the lake,
While the Fauna turns to Flora
In the hurricane aurora
That the phoenicopters make.

Mysteries of Roan and Sable,
By my magic, I was able
To decipher out of hand,
When the sunrise found me single
With my manuscript of shingle
And my lexicon of sand.

Now my skyline is a wall,
And these letters that I scrawl
Are the only tracks I study,
Dotted down in black and white,
For the phoenicopter's flight
I can find no blaze more ruddy

Than my deep, black flagon streams
Bleeding, over blank, white reams,
From its heart, that seems to glow
(Gnashed by the swordplay of the candle
That spurns the gloom with wingèd sandal)
Like sunrise on a field of snow. . . .

Or sunset on a sheet of sand
Where, stalking Pegasus, my hand
Nooses with rhyme the running line,
While the hushed words, with spoor of ink
Like wingèd zebras, come to drink
The still reflection of the wine.

Still I go trailing phantom herds—
Ideas, that take the form of words
And on the blank sheet leave their spoor:
Or swerve into a wild stampede,
Momentous in their strength and speed,
Till with the hieroglyphs they score.

The white page blackens; words of fire
Char with their hoofs each sheeted quire
While hot thoughts scorch upon their track,
As when, by whitest rays shot through,
The sky, so bright that it is blue,
Becomes so blue that it is black.

In the black hearts of wine and ink
The spectrum hides; for when to drink
I tilt the flagon—swiftly-wheeling,
The lit cup swirls with ruby fire
That wings its phoenicopter-gyre
Reflected round the walls and ceiling.

In that twinned blackness glint the gleams
Of certainties behind our dreams,
Which fire my hopes, since I have seen
Papyrus into words ignite
More proudly, when its leaves were white
Than into birds, when it was green!

★

The Singing Hawk

We thought his name a myth of native lore,
One of those tales to which the Bantu cling.
Yet what else could have swerved us from the spoor
Of lions, but so rare and strange a thing?—

What Hermes Trismegistus longed to hear,
The voice of light transmuted into sound,
And those who first approached the stratosphere
Heard on their brazen gondola rebound!

Before the sunrise, up the solar gradient,
The wingéd trumpet rose to flare and sing,
Like David's soul, triumphant, pure, and radiant,
When he had slain Goliath with his sling.

As if an eagle multiplied the lark's
Beatitude, a thousand times as strong,
Down from the frontiers to Lourenço Marques,
Horizons set no limits to his song.

Was it some trickery of the sense, we queried—
A light that sounded, or a sound that shone?
For like a blue Shekinah, still unwearied,
His voice kept blazing when his form was gone.

We could not tell if it was showering rays,
Or music rushed cascading from on high,
All that was certain was that it was praise,
And Gloria in Excelsis filled the sky.

Like a swift liner, churning into stars,
The drowsy phosphorous, till all the deep
Seems spangled with the music of guitars—
His song aroused the azure from its sleep.

The morning sky intensified its blue
Till brilliancy seemed gloom—an Arctic night
For that wild voice to flake with dancing flame
And wave with fiery streamers of delight.

His joy rolled out in infinite expansion
As when, at sea, huge suns in thunder die,
The wine-dark waves, in hexametric scansion,
Gallop with roaring manes along the sky.

As when through echoing canyons, crags, and fells
(Of all my ragged odysseys the goal)
Toledo prays, capsizing all her bells
While Salves soar, and hallelujahs roll—

His valour made the sad, black clouds rejoice
Climbing the Berg, though thick with hail and snow.
Though now for the first time I heard his voice,
Deep in my heart I'd felt him long ago.

Instinctively I felt him, as I feel
The absent reins within my empty hand,
And ghostly spurs that jingle at my heel,
When limping down the Broadway or the Strand.

He was the self-same ardour and vibration
That charged the fierce electrons of my breath
To fulminate the laughing imprecation
Which saved Andromeda from worse than death.

I felt his feathers stirruping my ankle
When, raising the Medusa's head above,
I saw the girl-fed Monster cringe, and crankle,
And wilt, before the wingéd sword of Love!

Oh warrior-bird! To make me more than rich,
Shed me a single feather for my pen!
Your war-song is the selfsame song with which
The Stars of Morning sang their first Amen.

High time for song (the prayer of sprightly wits)
When cowards shriek that Nothingness is nigh!
Though it were true—the Universe in bits—
That song would reassemble in the sky.

Those dances are the gayest which the sharp
Spurs clash to, while the jingled sabres ring.
Your revelry is such, you feathered harp!
Your talons are remembered, though you sing.

Between delight and valour there's no boundary.
Through silver peals the nerves of steel rebel.
Iron and silver, in the clanging foundry
Of your sole beak, are married—sword and bell.

These days the singer has to be a fighter:
The honey must be guarded by the sting:
And though you live for song, you are a smiter,
A hunter, and a sword upon the wing!

Pour down your songs of mingled wine and fire!
When raptures clash is when they best accord
To mate, as in your thunder-wingéd lyre,
Hosannas, and the honing of a sword.

AUTHOR'S NOTE: This is not a fable. I heard and saw this rare bird (whose existence is acknowledged by naturalists under the name of *Melierax Musicus*) while hunting last year in Portuguese East Africa.

★

Orpheus
(For Gene Tunney)

Now in his ninth reincarnation
the rubbernecked, Hell-touring Thracian,
    whom swivelling his headlamps cost
        his gender and the dame he lorded,
by one jerk of his ball-and-socket
thrown out of heart and mind and pocket—
    came back to sing for all he'd lost,
        and this is what the disk recorded.

Where State-Police dared scarcely follow,
with other herdsmen of Apollo,
    by my own solar sire employed
        I ran a bareboned enterprise,
out in the great wide open spaces,
those yawns of boredom on the faces
    of continents, so vast and void
        they seem to swallow up the skies.

126

Where Sirius in cypher flashes,
(a mitrailleur of dots and dashes),
   his morse of green and crimson fires
    whose messages must not be told—
decoding the forbidden words
I sang them to my starving herds,
   the stock of Seven Deadly Sires
    whom only harmony can hold.

The charm restrained each restive beast
whose red horns, sickled in the East,
   Though in the future participle,
    are lunar to the pending flood
wherein they gaze, portending famine,
a Pharaoh's nightmare to examine
   reflected in the last red ripple
    of daylight, as they drink its blood.

Astrologers of standard stars
(assassins of the blind guitars
   whose golden strings they snarled and tangled)
    Spoke only of expected slaughters,
but when of mine I stroked the strings
the four blue halcyons spread their wings,
   upon the sky my score was spangled
    And taught me by the winds and waters.

Dire snakes their deadly inclination
and rills, renouncing gravitation,
   exchanged their wonted ways and wills
    to the persuasion of my lyre:
for rills, like serpents fair and fond
enchanted by the charmer's wand,
   and deadly snakes, like harmless rills,
    rippled their loops of liquid fire.

Trees marched behind me as I played
and that's how avenues were made—
   by dryads falling into line.
    whole forests felled themselves in ranks,

told off from right to left by number,
then launched themselves as floating lumber
    upon my song (fir, spruce, and pine,)
        then sawed and stacked themselves in planks.

The more I sang, they pulped themselves
the more, to load the groaning shelves
    of bookshops, taking up positions,
        to hit the headlines in the News,
with trunks and boughs in pulp dissolving,
and rolls of linotype revolving,
    to foliate in fresh editions
        and fell themselves in foul reviews.

From underground my music drew
used oilshafts which were sawn into
    a million socket-holes, to sprout
        telegraphy—a pole in each.
Just with a rectilinear sound
I straightened roads that swerved and wound.
    to curve a bay I walked about,
        instead of straight along, the beach.

To tame the brutes of earth and seas
my later shipmates—Hercules,
    Jason, and Pollux—all confessed
        their methods fell far short of mine.
My livelihood, bull, horse, and whale
insured for years (this is no tale!)
    when I was hunted like a pest
        for swerving from the Party Line.

The Spaniards called me sticking-plaster.
I stuck so hard his tricks to master
    that Pegasus bucked off his brand
        and kicked his hind-shoes from the shell.
Upon his rump it left these scars
and my initials in the stars.
    As for his shoes, though forged by hand,
        they're kicking round the stars as well.

'Twas there I found the Truth (Eureka!)
and when the Reds had fired Guernica
  stripped stark the huge earthquaking Lie
    by entering with the first platoon
to save two-thirds of the doomed village,
which Herod, red with rape and pillage,
  swore had been blasted from the sky
    into a crater of the moon.

I sang that Fraud conditions all things
that Nations feel in great or small things,
  sage artist, gossip, tout, and barber
    fall for the selfsame doctored dope,
noosed in the same hypnotic lasso
that sprawled Neruda and Picasso.
  (Guernica, Badajoz, Pearl Harbour
    are slipknots in the same old rope!)

Incensed at its perspicuous presage,
the State Police condemned my message
  and, seeing I was past enslaving,
    condemned me with the dead to dwell,
for scorning vice, deriding devils,
with angels holding lawless revels—
  and gave me thus a chance for saving
    Eurydice from worse than Hell.

I dodged the first outlying pickets
and in the Subway took two tickets
  from Elephant and Castle station,
    whence I had started off before,
for loss had left me less a lubber,
and time had vulcanised the rubber
  and shelled with something more crustacean
    The vertebrae that veered of yore.

Gin-soaked, a shot-gun in her clutches,
the Fury was a future duchess
  whom Hell had posted for a sentry,
    and who, though in her periwig

the vipers, hissing vague alarm,
like neckties on a hawker's arm
   were faintly fluttered by my entry,
    continued snoring like a pig.

Although I lulled her snakes to sleep,
her elephants at bay to keep
   I did not need, for truth to tell
    she was not of the kind who've known
either Pink Elephants or Green,
but rather by such Beasts are seen
   when they are feeling far from well
    and have queer nightmares of their own

With Charon's outboard grimly chugging,
the armless torso closely hugging
   of my guitar, I made the landing
    at Lambeth on the Lesbian shore:
and from that Hell of English whoredom,
dead vice, and dull provincial boredom,
   my former failures notwithstanding,
    the fond Eurydice I bore.

When on the bank we tried to land
and found that both of us were banned,
   the land to me became a lock
    to which the ocean was the key,
and, signing on before the mast,
why, surely I was not the last,
   when doubt had foundered on a rock,
    to found my faith upon the sea.

And so to beat their curst embargo
dovetailing Pequod, Ark, and Argo,
   new world, gold fleece, and mystic whale,
    I made my faith one ship, quest, cargo,
course, compass, quadrant, guiding star,
and whatsoever doom avail
   the hazard of my questing sail—
    reef, solitude, or floating spar.

With hempen harpstrings tautly shrouded,
the oread sisters, thunderclouded
   with cumulus of straining cloth,
      sang to me with their souls of pine,
while harpers with the waves for strings
feathered them with their silver wings
   whose quills were oars, whose down was froth,
      to swan my Argoes through the brine.[1]

The pines strode forward as I played,
whether in stately colonnade
   on slopes of Alp or Guadarrama
      or the sierras of the main
on decks as steep. Stampeding herds
taught me the impetus of words:
   and all I ever learned of drama
      was in the Catacombs of Spain.

There when I slew the Tcheka's warder
and sentry, in that brief disorder,
   did I a second time from Hell come
      escaping, too, the common char-pit,
but lost the crown of the elected
by my unworthiness rejected,
   when guns, to bid the martyrs welcome,
      spread for those kings a crimson carpet.

In me, with dextral whorl, the Mistral
and the Sirocco, with sinistral
   volution, wrestling meet, to pull
      from strife the absolute accord,
depending on antagonism
to dynamise my dancing rhythm,
   as on the matador the bull
      whose consummation is the sword.

   I know all victories are vain
   to that which I beheld in Spain

---

[1] Actually the Portuguese Cod-Fleet which still uses sail and oars for
individual fishing, off Newfoundland.

where with the eagle mates the dove
　　the might of armies to defy
Since with Euridyce's recapture,
I crossed the Rubicon of rapture,
　　I'll ask no more of life, nor love.
　　　　It is my death for which I die—

A death of blood and tears as cruel
as could hydrate the blazing jewel
　　of faith from ashes reascendant
　　　　with which the victors rose resplendent,
when love with love fought out the duel
both as the fire and as the fuel,
　　son, father, ancestor, descendant,
　　　　and phoenix of its own renewal! . . .

Just here his voice was overheard
and he was taken at his word
　　which cut short the recording session:
　　　　and when the State Police had got him,
after the regulation season
of torture, when he lost his reason,
　　no autocritical confession
　　　　could be extracted. So they shot him.

Dedicatory Epilogue to Rob Lyle

Our dead want company. Friends go off daily
First it was Dylan Thomas, then Tschiffely,
And now its Regimental Sergeant Major
Mulvey. The next I would not care to wager
But worse than death, a hundred times, is vice
For turning friends to carrion in a trice.
Death's but a tyro to the Booktrade, surely,
For turning men to corpses prematurely:
Their sprites, long lost, a darker doom controls
Who for their reputations gave their souls,
Corrupted or conniving in the game
That dooms their Race to slavery or shame
If not Annihilation from Above,
The fate of all who play the fool with Love!
As Sodom and Gomorrah proved too true,
The Incas and the Aztecs lived to rue,
And Rome and Babylon can witness too.
Whether the chosen agent of Destruction
Be plague or famine, earthquake or eruption,
Conquistador, like Cortes or Pizarro,
Or Commissar, more bigoted and narrow,
Or, worse than all, a snowy-haired professor,
Of a neat violin the fond possessor,
To fiddle when it all goes up in flames,[1]
The crime is one: the sentence is the same!

Now only you and I remain alive
Of that convivial, oddly-sorted five—
Yet not so strangely, being forced as males,
Like five bulls facing outward from our tails,
In self-defence of our forbidden gender
To band together, rather than surrender
Our manhood to the All-Castrating Knife
Of London and its literary life.
But, that there "be no moaning at the bar"
Here or in heaven, or where else they are,
First let us pledge those comrades staunch and true
And next, my dearest friend, I drink to you

[1] "I pressed the button." (Einstein, on hearing of Hiroshima.)

In the same juice you trod with me together
Last year; it flows like life-blood from the leather
Of my fat wineskin swinging from the fork
Of this old tree so smoothly stripped of cork,
Reminding us of you, for when you stayed
With us, we used to share its fragrant shade.
The pines are hushed, before the first lone star
Changes from gold to blue. Our soft guitar
Spangles the stillness with its five taut rays
As when upon a stream the sunlight plays.
Then the frog's voices, far less heard than seen,
Freckle the hush with tiny dots of green
Encouraging the Stars. The fireflies weave
Their burning stitches through the silken sleeve
Of our lit watercourse that, very soon,
Will reach an arm to pluck the setting moon.
The owls relieve the orioles in the limes,
The nightingales each other: and the chimes
Ring through the breeze which leagues of orange bloom
Scent through. The far-off breakers faintly boom
Six miles away on Europe's westernmost,
And steepest cape of all its rugged coast,
Where Boreas sounds his foghorn in the crags
To barcarolle the cormorants and shags.
These verses that I here compose at random
In couplets (my old customary tandem)
Are just to make a present of the rest,
Forming this book, to my Arcadian guest.
By your first tracks in verse I could decode
That a young lion had just crossed the road,
Ahead of me. This knowledge by the herd
Of Fame-Castrated oxen, word by word,
Was faithfully translated without flaw—
In silence, which is eloquent of awe—
Shame fills each literary catamite
Who stands aghast at beauty and delight,
But here I crown you with my own green bays
Whom I was first to recognise and praise.
From your ex-sergeant, still your comrade too,
My Captain and my Godson, here's to you!

134

Flowering Rifle

A Poem from the "Battlefield of Spain"

(Dedicated to Mary Campbell)

"Perhaps I had better inform my Protestant readers that the famous dogma of papal infallibility is by far the most modest profession of its kind in existence. Compared to our infallible democracies, our infallible medical councils, our infallible astronomers, our infallible Parliaments, the Pope is on his knees in the dust confessing his ignorance before God."

GEORGE BERNARD SHAW

"The science to which I pinned my faith is bankrupt. Its tales were more foolish than all the miracles of the priests. . . . What it spread was not an enlightenment but a malignant disease. Its counsels, which should have established the millennium, have led directly to the suicide of Europe. I believed them once more whole-heartedly than any religious fanatic believed his superstitions; for in their name I helped to destroy the faith of the millions of worshippers in the temples of a thousand creeds.

GEORGE BERNARD SHAW

Author's Note Added to Proofs in September 1938

THIS poem was written before Mr. Chamberlain interrupted the disastrous course of English foreign politics herein satirized:[1] and the manuscript has been out of my reach most of the time since. I hope this will excuse what might otherwise seem congenital pessimism and ingratitude for not alluding to the event. But before that it was difficult enough for born Englishmen to feel very patriotic, let alone for South Africans like myself! I therefore retain the original diatribe for its bearing on the decisive part of the Spanish War and also as a talisman against any relapse into suicidal hysterics on the part of British foreign policy, since Democracy is so subject to war-psychosis. How far at sea the Russian experts and their British satellites were about Spain there is no need for me to rub in. The bulk of my Spanish "War Poems" were printed in England two or three years before the war, and the last one to appear, early in 1935 (in *Time and Tide* of all places) clearly symbolized the Spanish war in a nutshell, together with the Red Debacle—"The Fight." These poems (with the exception of four on Toledo inserted in the proofs) were sent in before the war and appeared as a book in the first weeks of the war, predicting the Red Debacle at a time when the British "Intelligentsia" was celebrating a Soviet triumph, so they were not very popular. They were treated as the work of a romantic, and excused on "literary grounds" for being on the spot (as usual) about ten years before the British Intelligentsia! In this book, naturally, I have still refused to wear the compulsory intellectual uniform of the British "Intelligentsia," however romantic it may seem of me to walk upright instead of crawling about on all fours in the mental outfit of a moth-eaten Beefeater: and I have every hope that this work will appear as strange to them as my last, for events are anachronizing them so quickly that they can only continue to exist by intensifying the make-believe and unreality of their world, and by increasing their overtures to death, or, more belatedly, to birth-control ("not to be born")—for their spiritual self-abortionism shows

[1] This refers to the half-hearted attempt at Munich to avert the present fate of Europe.

them to be more at home in the "Au Delà" than ever they will be in this life.

Humanitarianism, their ruling passion, an erzatz substitute for charity, invariably sides where there is most room for sentimental self-indulgence in the filth or famine of others. It sides *automatically* with the Dog against the Man, the Jew against the Christian, the black against the white, the servant against the master, the criminal against the judge. It is a suicidal form of moral perversion due to overdomestication, protestantism gone bad, just as are the other perversions with which our intellectuals are riddled. It was natural that it should side with the party that has slaughtered almost as many unarmed victims in the rearguard as the whole war has yet slain (with battles, sieges, air raids, and our executions) of soldiers and civilians alike.[1] It is as helpless in front of propaganda as a frozen tadpole in front of a boaconstrictor: and propaganda is the Red's main arm. Like all English writers on Spain I am biassed, but not by this form of sentimental perversion. I am biassed, unlike any of the others, by a thorough first-hand experience of life under both régimes as one of the working population: by the price and quality of bread: by the filth and famine obtaining on the side which started with the entire Capital of the country and the richest lands: and by the record-breaking harvests and prosperity on the side which only has the Labour—pulverizing any pretensions of the "left wing" to represent the Spanish worker, who can produce double of everything (where that paralysing influence is removed) with only half the amount of hands: thereby proving, according to the Marxian standards of *productivity*, that the Marxist is an anachronism and an economical drag on the country, who even in his own paradise has sunk far, far beneath the lowest level of pre-war republican production and should be (*according to his own lights*) "liquidated" forthwith, as an unproductive "mouth," and a parasitic belly. He is fortunate to have more merciful judgment. This poem does not attempt to emulate such fine writers as Claudel and Pemán, who have done justice to the Epic and Lyrical aspects of the Spanish Renaissance. This is simply an account in terms of everyday life, from my own experience at the front and in both rearguards, of what must be the most extraordinary awakening of a national consciousness in a ruined and prostrate country that the world has yet seen.

[1] The Reds subsequently killed almost as many of their own side as they did of Nationalists.

Book I

A hundred years of strife with warring vans
Had winnowed Spain in two distinctive clans
Upon the left, inflammable, the chaff,
Corn to the right, the vulnerable half,
And thus in Spanish history began
The war between the Wowser and the Man—
Him that through tortoise-shell the rainbow saw
And ate his breakfast through a dead man's jaw,[1]
Who over lenses droops his godless lugs,
To regulate his life by those of bugs,
And whether it would better them or not,
Upon all others would impose his lot:
To figures who would subjugate our souls,
And hold a meeting when the tempest rolls,
By dead statistics would control a city
And run a battleship with a committee:
Though through the world wherever he prevailed,
His meddlesome experiments have failed:
Whether at work by the Infernal Lake,
He urge the world to war for peace's sake
Like a snug lawyer fostering the Feuds
From which his slimy livelihood exudes,
Or godless surgeon in a sinecure
Who farms the cancers he pretends to cure,
And at all costs will keep the sickness sound
With busy Mafias working underground:
But when by pulling wires and licking stamps
The nearest to his victory he ramps,
And (history can testify the rule)
Would leap into the saddle from his stool
The bronco Life, with angry snort of fire,
Has ever boomeranged four feet entire
And stamped him like a cockroach in the mire.
Upon the Right his would-be victim stood,
Armed chiefly with a sense of Bad and Good,

[1] Wowser is any kind of puritan killjoy, socialist and fabian, or pedant.
There is a prophetic inkling here of the close bond between false teeth
and socialism—before Bevan's "buckshee" dentures were heard of.

Who had retained erect his classic form
Through all the epidemics of Reform:
Catastrophes of progress failed to bow
His haughty gaze and heaven-seeking brow:
His mother wit rejected any movement
That bid him cut his throat for self-improvement,
Nor would he hack away his legs or arms
Because his sires had used them on the farms:
Whose life's a Georgic orderly and clean,
Who long has learned what dud reformers mean,
Shrewd in philosophy the fraud to scout,
In labour proud, in worship most devout,
Who reads less nonsense from his running brooks
Than waiters, primer-proud, with knowing looks,
Can mumble out of newspapers and books.
Who scorns the bargains of the soul-contractor,
To give his horse up for the Common Tractor,
And slave beneath a fiscal or a Factor,
Who've got the Russian clown Ju-jitsu'd clean,
Whom they can starve and trample and demean
By shutting off his store of gasolene:
The Russian was a savage: he of Spain
More highly civilized and deeply sane
Than most who read the papers in the train,
Was first the foreign heresy to hate,
On his broad shoulders fell the bloody spate
But only proved as many times before,
The Man of Peace is terrible in war!
He had a private spirit of his own
Nor pined for letting other folk alone,
But he would fight to keep his home entire
Although it was the devil lit the fire:
In him you have the Adversary, Man,
Go Hammer him according to your plan
And geld him with a Sickle if you can!
And that he took not kindly to the chain
Well may the baffled demagogues complain
Who never knew the Eagle Heart of Spain,
Nor nearer came to her dark eyes or hair
To see the deeps of splendour burning there,

Than to some bolshy "meeting" in the Square—
Nor guessed how high she lifts her peerless head
Whose burning saints on cold and hunger fed:
And, since the pain and sorrow of the world
Was far too soft a pillow, fiercely hurled
Their empire to the ends of the Abyss,
Searching the gulfs of the subconscious mind
New fiends to conquer, continents to find,
And ray their thoughts like comets to the blind:
Who face to face would meet with fiery beams
The eyeless monsters that molest our dreams
To show the way they can be faced and routed—
And Freud, the pervert's Bible, gaily flouted.
All his worst nightmares they had foxed from earth
And hunted down—an age before his birth,
When the subhuman dream, to its derision,
Confronted by the clear seraphic vision,
Shrunk like a squid: and left the wakened sprite
To sun its clouds with valour and delight—
All our psychology so damp and dreary,
By practice mastered, where we grope with theory,
By conquest answered, where we pose the query—
Where ours leave off by darkness circled in,
Their terrible discoveries begin,
And far across the line where we draw rein
Their fiery beacons light the fearful plain,
Over the wreck of battles fiercely won,
The vanguard and the outposts of the Sun!
Was this the race that could be tamely fed
On the Utopian blarney of the Red,
Or bribed to trade its devil-daring breath
For slavery, equality, and death:
And, if these lying promises were truth,
For cheaper bread renounce its flaming youth—
Or the religion of the heart and head
For that of the soft belly and its bread?

Though "Pity the poor Reds" is now the cry
To greet our hard-won conquest of the sky,
When with our cities blown about our ears

We bore in silence what they bawl in tears
Before we had a bomber fledged to fly,
And months before we ventured to reply;
And bombs seemed respite to their thirsty knives
When young and old with half a million lives
Defrayed their clinic rage of G.P.I.
Whose Freudian delirium slew more
Than on both sides the heavy toll of war
And robbed the graves lest souls in peace should lie,
To whose main swamp and tidal wave of blood
The war seemed less a tributary flood
Than channel sluiced to drain that welter dry
Which still, in Russia, after twenty years,
Undrained, a stagnant fever-swamp appears,
And here, unconduited, would reek as high:
But that in Spain has waked a different breed
The murder-thriving bureaucrats to weed,
Who only prune themselves to multiply,
For all the rage of battles, sieges, bomb-raids,
Falls short of the Humanitarian "Comrades"
To whom the cowed and crowded cities yield
More room for prowess than the open field.
This will be seen when Triumph clears the sky
With Nitre less obscured than by the Lie,[1]
Lenin's "Most Powerful Weapon" (as he boasts)
To sow hysteria to the farthest coasts
Exasperating multitudes to die;
Then who this Glorious Rising would forgo?
Since Nature rose, Herself, the way to show
On her defacers raining blow for blow:
Corn, out of shame, refused for them to grow
And Gold (the looted wealth of all the land)
Inured to theft by every filthy hand,
The dirtiest of the elements in chief,
That loves the chill, webbed hand-clasp of the thief,
Its abject soul no further could demean
When Villainy and Fraud were swindled clean,
But rushed their frontiers headlong from a scene

[1] "Used with skill, the Lie can be forged into our most powerful weapon." Lenin.

Where forces nameless yet in books of crime
Had broken from the padded cells of Time.
Daring the rage of all who vainly think
Against a Nation to uphold a Stink,
In the fat snuggery of Auden, Spender,
And others of the selfsame breed and gender,
Who hold by guile the fort of English letters
Against the final triumph of their betters,
Muzzle the truth, and keep the Muse in fetters[1]
While our own hoary sages with white hairs
Must cringe to them, like waiters on the stairs,
And few but Wyndham Lewis and myself,
Disdain salaaming for their praise and pelf,
With cleansing bombs to air the stuffy dens
Wherein they pick their noses with their pens,
Once more in naked blasphemy I stalk
And dare to prove I am not made of pork,
To flaunt this flaming heresy, the Truth,
Before the senile owl-roosts of our youth
Whom monkeys' glands seem powerless to restore,
As Birth Control was profitless before,
Which, sponsored by their mockery of a Church,
Like stranded barbels, left them in the lurch,
Whose only impact on the world's affairs
Has been to cause a boom in Rubber shares,
Who come to battle with both arms held up
And ask to be invited home to sup—
While back at home, to sound their battle-horn,
Some self-aborted pedants stray forlorn
And pity those who venture to be born—
Born, if they knew it, in the Morning's pride
When never Death was sweeter to deride
Nor Life so fresh and fiery for the ride.
They gasp, or yawn, to see in splinters hurled
Their Meetingoid, Committee-bungled world
Crushed with the self-same weapons that they chose
Their dogmatized Utopias to impose,

[1] This refers to all the meetings and manœuvres of the left-wing
poets to ban and boycott the "Georgiad", now a classic, and this poem
—which soon will be.

Those Hells on Earth, against whose gloom we soldier,
That put in practice, turned out ten times mouldier
Than Dartmoor, Wormwood Scrubs, or Comrades' Hall,
And which we have abolished once for all:
But which, while they'd the least pretence to shape,
Even dunghill rats surveyed with bristled nape
And dared the wildest torrents to escape:
For never yet was loafing such a passion
Or murder, rape, and arson so in fashion
As where conjoined in Brotherhood of "Labour"
Humanitarian Progress loves its Neighbour,
The bloated Cæsars in their purple lists
Out-Cæsared by to-day's Philanthropists
Who, in as many weeks as they took years,
Trebled Rome's catacombs for blood and tears:
Who slaughter ten times more, their love to press,
Than we for anger, vengeance, or redress,
No less when on each other's necks they fall
And then they are most "comradely" of all,
Through the dark streets pursue their bestial "work"
And "labour" with the pistol and the dirk,
Till their own press, so used to deeds of mirk,
Despairs of these humanitarian brothers
And pleads for intercession—to their Mothers!
And though the hate of parents what it preaches,
To Christian Decency abjectly screeches—
A "crime" they'll punish with far worse than death,
Yet for whose aid they gasp at every breath—
When we return their bombs, or "Freedom" hangs
Too heavy on their scruffs with gory fangs,
Depending on the creed they most abhor
And cadging all the time for more and more.
Never before by earthquake, fire or tide
Were bankruptcy or famine spread so wide
As by this all-reforming modern State
That voted work and eating out of date,
Whose best reform in labour, food, or pelf,
Has been that it anachronized itself.
While we, worse-handicapped, without a dime,
Fought and created in the teeth of time,

Who had no programme, years before prepared,
But had to snatch the moment as it flared.
With our spare hand (which they reserve for plunder)
Fixed to the Plough, and in our Right, the thunder,
Victorious in the harvest as the strife
We fly our banner on the Staff of Life,
Against their looted Mammon to sustain
A bronzed and curling Samson in the grain,
Whose lovely shocks more terrible appear
Than if with dragons' teeth we'd sowed the rear,
A golden army waving through the land
Though fringed with scarlet war on either hand,
With her own flag of red and golden flame
The exiled, homing country to reclaim,
We spread upon her smoked and blackened limbs
The fleece of glory where the morning swims.
Like shells in quantity, as theirs in kind,
Whose bread's as black and leaden as their mind,
The silver loaves our ammunition swell,
And shining stoves are armaments as well,
Since of the mortal kind it's ours to capture
As much, or more, than we can manufacture
And twice our Works have ceased to turn a shell
As when Alfambra broke, Bilbao fell,
The dumps were piled so high that to the sight
It seemed the peaks had calved them overnight;
Though the Reds grow most valiant in their writing
When lack of arms excuses them from fighting,
Many besides myself have touched no gun
Or cutlery, but what from them was won.
If in most modern wars both sides are beaten,
Here no such platitudes we fight to sweeten—
Where both sides gain, though one against its will,
Cured of its madness by the surgeon's skill:
The pruning sword conveys a hydra gift
And tendrils flower from every clog we shift,
And where it lopped the paralytic lump
A Briareus branches from the stump:
Like paralytics from their trances cured
Who leap to life at Fatima or Lourdes:

With style to compensate for deadweight lost
Creative rhythm thrice repays the cost
And thaws numbed strikers from their year-round frost:
Like trade winds to the stale and stagnant calms,
Dexterity releases lock-jawed palms,
And freshening runs to each suspended hand
As wanted rain through blistered forks of sand.
For there's no Spaniard, Falangist or Red,
That can be driven, or that can't be led—
It's the Red Fields they still refuse to till
Though Chekas thunder, and their bloodhounds kill—
But on our side the barns are filled to burst,
And those that blame it on "coercion" first
Should find the Spaniard that can be coerced:
Only in Propaganda he appears
To chuck the Witch and Ogre from their spheres,
Wherever pommies lend their blood-red ears.
If damned coercion could have ruled the land
I would not hold this rifle in my hand,
But have to strike and dawdle half the year
Lest work offend the loafing pistoleer,
Or only work at such a wage and board
As no one in the country could afford—
For if you jibbed you'd only hear a thud
And if you woke at all, would wake in blood.
The votes, as if Democracy to slight,
And show its rusted workings to the sight,
Seated the left, yet counted for the right—
And this in spite of violated urns,
Shots at the booths, and falsified returns;
And straight the sinister and bungling drone
Prepared to cut its partner from the bone—
The dexterous hand was threatened for its life
By its tight-fisted vixen of a wife,
To whom that drunken judgement passed the knife:
And like Petruchio (had his wife been worse)
Must fence unarmed against his wedded curse;
And soon her cuts had opened wide the vein—
Our pull in numbers through the Terror's reign
Adjusted by some half a million slain—

And loud they boasted, ere their tails were curled,
Their purpose was to sweep us from the world!
Though for five months we'd turned the other cheek
And when we struck, with loss of blood were weak,
Too late alas to stop the coward hand
That struck the hope and honour of the land
Who promised fair to parallel the Star,
Triumphant, of the gracious Salazar,
And only just in time to stay the wave
That would have swept the country to its grave
With all of Europe after, had it grown
And Spain not dared the fearful tide alone.
Such foreign aid as, later, we were lent,
The Reds already to the front had sent,
Out-numbering still, to-day, by four to one,
And antedating with four months to run:
Only the mad, Red populace was armed,
And well the weeded Army had been farmed,
Or "triturated," in Azaña's phrase—
A four-eyed Janus squinting divers ways,
With the Red generals in the pride of place
And ours consigned to exile and disgrace:
And though the whole Armada jilted thus,
Save for the fifth of it that stayed with us,[1]
It crystallized the whole tremendous scene
Wherein the miracle's less clearly seen,
But here the Lie's restricted in its might
By Daylight, on the borders of the fight,
And cannot vent its squidlike screen of ink
As where the thunderclouds obscure the blink—

[1] It is a curious thing that English poets always have to misrepresent
the side they support as being a plucky little fellow standing up to a
great big bully, however many times that side may outnumber the
other. To read Day Lewis's "Little Nabara" gives this impression.
Similarly English poems on the Armada gave the impression that the
gross tonnage and number of ships, contrary to the truth, was on
the Spanish side. Tonnage was equal in the battle which finally swept the
sea of the English slave traders and pirates, Cobham and Brooke and
cost Drake's life and Raleigh's and Hawkin's liberty. The Spaniards
never called their fleet the "Invincible Armada". Though the English
ships were smaller, they outnumbered the foe in a proportion of 19-13.

Where in the Ports the part blockades the Whole,
Dead bulk out-marshalled by the fiery soul:
The sea reflecting in its glassy frame
Both politics and strategy the same,
Upholds a mirror of the War we win
To those who get no insight from within—
As I who've lived beneath the two regimes
And have not dreamed the Leftie Teacher's dreams,
Being no tourist, but with working hand
Curled in the mane of that equestrian land,
One with what was eternal in that Nation
To bear its woes with silent resignation
Until the choice was suicide or War:
For in her Cosmopolitan furore
Spain was a mirror in a public place
Where every stranger, seeing his own face,
Especially if it was botched or sore,
Believed it for the land that we Restore
His pimples for her kopjes he mistook
And for her Church his nose's monstrous hook:
Her womanhood for his contagious whore—
And of his own reflection made a book:
Since the Real Spain was in the cloisters hidden
Beneath the fiery sky on mesas ridden
Where tourists would have fainted with the heat—
It was her dregs that filtered to the street,
Where communism hung around the bars
Among the dominoes and cheap cigars,
Where waiters, chauffeurs, menials were the guys
That headed on the infernal enterprise.
Let such as Bartlett blame their lack of spelling
For the subhuman crime he finds repelling,
Not on the damned philosophy he preaches
That mostly through the press its feelers reaches:
Do Bushmen or Bechuanas fall so low
Though on their Baobabs no primers grow?
It was the literate lounging class of Spain
That first conceived this Rabies of the brain.
The hardest workers, those that read the least,
Could still distinguish Beauty from the Beast—

The dope-fiends of cheap literature are first
To get their notions by the Kremlin cursed,
And reading without wisdom is to blame
For half the world destroyed with blood or flame—[1]
By Left-wing reading incapacitated
Either to tolerate or be tolerated.
Experience better serves the most Unread
Who carry no Boloney home to bed.
But in her outward structure as it stood
While foreign borers criticized the wood
Which they themselves had chewed into a cud:
Amongst its crazy scaffolds, stays and props,
Quack-carpentered, and "jerried" in the shops,
I felt the living wood that was to bud,
Intact, with all the blossoms in its blood,
The upright stem, the horizontal spars,
That flowered so red to fruit in deathless stars,
But then as in the grasp of winter stood:
In all that buckled hulk of creaking wood,
It was the Cross that strangers had forgot
The only beam that did not smell of rot
But fragrant as a rose-tree after rain:
That though it was to take the hardest strain
Of all the girders in her width and length,
Subjected to the self-same test of strength,
After the fire and tempest, would remain
Eternal, where all else collapsed and gave,
Starred in her sky, or rooted on her grave—
Giving their own advantages and odds
To the cash-counting, belly-bolstered gods
And leaving them, when they had won the toss,
Brained by the thundering hammer of the Cross!
Knowing these things how could I entertain
The Charlies' Meeting Bates mistook for Spain,
Whose false experience of the land must yield
To mine both in the letters as the field:

[1] I notice that Bertrand Russell made the same statement about
fifteen years after, and ten years too late. Nothing, no idea or thought is
ever allowed to come out of the bag in England or U.S. until it has lost
impetus or interest.

Or take like Hemingway for "Spanish Earth"
Her richest acres decimating dearth,
Whose chiefs to beg for foreign corn must go
Which her best workers still refuse to grow—
Unless they have been murdered long ago:
While on our side the harvest has been rolled,
Brave as a lion with its mane of gold,
Up to the foremost trenches that we hold.
I saw the things that strike the tourist least—
Behind the bull-fighter, I saw the priest
More valiantly engage a vaster Beast,
With nobody to alternate or save,
Whose dark arena was the certain grave,
Who torried with the Fiend for crusts of bread
And took his final salary in lead.
For one, the gay peseta's jingling shower
Like rain in April, when the palcos flower,
Where snowed with powder, cataracting pearls,
And forested on high with jet-blue curls,
A whole sierra made of lovely girls,
Thundering with a pigeon-flight of hands,
Sheers to the zenith from the blood-lit sands—
The trumpet slashed, and as the people roared,
More strident than the trumpet pealed the sword!
But for the priest, alone to take his toss
And ride the red horns of his Master's cross
Amid the frenzy of demented scenes
And the worse slander of our fat black Deans,[1]
When each strong Hercules, to all but Love
Invincible, had by that stronger force
Been vanquished as an eagle tears a dove:
And victor of the iron was the Corse
When none recanted to deflect the blow
As twenty thousand martyrdoms can show!

[1] The apocryphal wealth of the Spanish Church is another English belief. The Church was destituted of property almost a century ago. Here is the scale of wealth:
Cardinal of Toledo's salary, £1,600; Archbishop of Canterbury, £15,000. 14,726 Spanish Parish Priests, £36 to 20 a year. 12,698 English Incumbents average £517. 1,711 Spanish Parish Priests £100 to 40 a year.

But I, for one, can't visualize a Dean
Fried, for intransigence, in gasolene:
What are the faults such valour is not worth
That as a penny spends his life on Earth.
To some I know, with foreign baksheesh sent,
Like bottled germs, to foster discontent,
And coolie-ing Russia, by such action,
To drive out mere decay with putrefaction
(Helping our cause, as surgeons help his heirs
Who kill the patient with their rival cares)
Spain was to them what scurf they could infect
And flake away with their bought intellect;
So with the Kominterners of the day,
Mistaking both the slough and the decay
In which as feeding parasites they lay
When with the withered skin they peeled away—
For the live python with revolving spires
That from the tombstone of her mighty sires,
Shedding the rags of winter-bitten skin
With the snug parasites that housed within,
Volted with solar glories and desires
And wheeled upon a hundred spangling tyres
To strip the Zodiac of its rolling fires,
With gleaming helmets for her million scales
From a long winter of inertia sails
In a strong current of electric might
Like a great river churning power and light.
From dynamos of valour and delight.
Across the land she flings her glorious wave,
Circles the deathless City of the Brave,
And floods the desert with reviving rain—
The Sweat and Blood of sufferers and slain,
That shed for love, was never shed in vain.
Now the lost Hammer wakens from its swoon
And the dead Sickle, like the crescent moon
On the deep sea (two horns for every wave),
Comes like the Resurrection from the grave
And through the swells of softly waving corn
In glinting lines (for every wave a horn)
Is with the warm wind of the harvest borne,

A million tons, a sickle for each ton,
Of surplus wheat, refulgent in the sun!
So in the Stock as in the garnered wheat,
A lost moon livens to the solar heat
To swell the herds like tides, each wave a beast,
Whose rippling fat's with gold and silver fleeced,
While surplus calves, with half a million brows,
Prepare the silver crescent to espouse,
Whose swelling horn the rest of Spain can feast.
The Bull, the massive Mountain on her plain,
The Hillrange of her work, the garnered grain:
Her two life-giving streams of wine and oil,
The Tagus and the Ebro of her toil:
The snowed sierras of her gathered Rice
That pearl in creamy height to fall in price—
Let these, her handwork, to the Earth and Sky
Proclaim the Worker's Spain against the Lie
Which all in quantities unknown of yore,
May justify the bloody purge of war,
Since loafing communists, the country's sore,
Had made such health impossible before:
Which, too, may compensate, for strangled vice,
The feelings of such literary lice
That fell off with such flakes of winter skin
They could infect or loosen from within,
When Spain threw down her dominoes and dice,
And Franco bade the epic years begin,
Flying unarmed to dare the fiery zone
And shouldering the Impossible alone,
To lift three fallen centuries from the slime
Where they had bogged the ebb and flow of time,
Which is no one-way stream as we mischart,
But circulates, like blood, the solar heart,
And when the artery's stopped, to sap the vein,
The sword must slice the ligature in twain.

Then five of our first leaders that were six[1]
Rushed forth to seize a bridgehead on the Styx,
On duty killed, or that they scorned to fly

[1] Sanjurjo's Franco, Mola, Calvo Sotelo, Goded, J. A. Primo de Rivera.

When for their blood was raised the wolfish cry
(Unlike Red chiefs, who scuttle to Valencia—
And after to Geneva—peradventure!);
And if our sixth survives to see us win
It was not shirking danger saved his skin,
But that he flew so boldly in her face
It jerked her Phrygian Nightcap out of place:
For with a buffet as he brushed her by,
And zoomed from Teneriffe into the sky,
It jerked the aim and focus from her eye.
Waiting in ambush these, the Fury hid
Her snaky topknot, like a lurking squid,
Within the crater's inky cloud of smoke,
And primed her snaky tresses for the stroke.
As when a gust, with truculent alarm,
Flutters the neckties on a hawker's arm,
Swirling their dots and spangles on the gale,
They all lash out and strike—to no avail;
So did her tentacles of snaky hair,
With idle fangs that chopped the empty air,
Strike out and miss him—parried by a prayer.
She wrenched a foothill then from Teide's base
And sent it flying after him through space.
The missile grazed the aviating chief
And seemed a meteor over Teneriffe,
Fell, hurtling on, it struck the brows of Spain
And, like the life-blood of her dearest vein,
The scarlet boinas[1] trickled to the plain,
Till all Navarre was sown with drops of red
And half Castile with seeds of blood was spread:
Like holly in the woodland budding blithe,
Were every thorn a pitchfork or a scythe:
Like poppies in the grasses they were seen
Were every blade a bayonet to have been—

[1] The Scarlet Berets of the Requetés—chiefly Basques—the famous
Carlist militia which saved Spain at the beginning of the Civil War,
when the army was disarmed and disorganized. And the Red Terror was
loosed on the defenceless populace. These civilians at the battle of
Oriamindi, in the last century, though without artillery, defeated a
British Regular Army under Gen. Sir Lacy Evans.

Home-made perhaps, but resolute and keen.
Those scarlet seeds took root in every field
Where Christ is King. An army was the yield.
Had they been dragons teeth and every tooth
Had sprung into a brave indignant youth
On fire to fight and die for Christ the King—
It would be less miraculous a thing.
For here were old men shuffling off to war
With muskets that a hundred years before
Routed Sir Lacy Evans from the shore
And captured his artillery outright
Whose Regulars refused to turn and fight
Although he raged and cursed with all his might.[1]
Rise up, you Cocks, like Requetés enrolled,
With your red *boinas* and your spurs of gold,
And crow the Dawn of Victory afar . . .
"The Requetés are rising in Navarre!"
To meet her Chief, his Rubicon the Straits,
His country rose—but to fling wide the gates:
The cry was not to challenge, but implore,
With which she shook the desolated shore:[2]
A headless phantom, she, in ragged attire
Whose flying streamers flogged the winds with fire,
Swung, like a lantern, her dismembered head
In which, like coals, the eyes were blazing red.
Those jet-blue curls that taught the grapes to grow
Had whitened in a night to hanks of snow,
With sleety whistle from her hand they spread
And seemed the smoke of that suspended head,
With which she turned to lamp him on his way
Through scenes of madness that defied the day—
Humanity, benighted at midnoon,
Had howled the sun into a small red moon,
And saw, through smoke, that high and holy light
As grey Baboons behold the moon at night.

[1] See General Sir Lacy Evans correspondence from San Sebastian with the War Office. His men were so badly broken that they refused to emerge from the fortifications again.

[2] Allusion to the tremendous passage in Lucan where Rome appears to Cæsar at the Rubicon, to try to stop him.

But with the Gorgon-beauty of her face,
Where the Medusa's would have chilled the race
Of blood, and walled the heart with chilling stone,
She turned his heart to adamant alone
Whose fiery crystal blazing from his breast,
The star of San Fernando,[1] saved the West.
But for her Master's wounds, with which she showed
The Signs of Resurrection on the road,
But for the Wounds upon her hands and feet—
The bravest would have sounded his retreat
Or plunged to suicide, to thunder down
With all creation for his tomb and crown.
Since, had not here the fury been withstood,
The world would have returned to rocks and wood,
With some few Anarchists to rake its crust
Who had not died of surfeit or disgust,
For such a fever as was here released,
But that its rage was quarantined and creased,
So ghoulishly babooning to the beast,[2]
Might well have swept the world! But Herbert Read
And Huxley, too, with tender hearts that bleed,
For corpse-defiling Anarchists must plead!
O world gone imbecile! each way one looks
Humanitarians slobbering over crooks!
Each skull a box of worms before its time,
To fish for bloaters of subhuman crime
In the backwaters of the Stygian gloom,—
Prawning for larvæ where the mildews bloom!
These in their lives, as in their prose and verse,
Anticipate the coffin and the hearse:
When living Christians have been fed to pigs,
The maggot never stirs beneath their wigs
As pleased as punch when half a million die

[1] The Spanish V.C. won in youth by Gens. Franco, Varela, Milan Astray, and Moscardò.

[2] At the end of "Seven Red Sundays", the spokesmen of the Republicans, Ramon Sender, ends that book with a pæan to the Red Terror (then impending) and gloatingly predicting orgies of "unspeakable crimes", a passage quoted with 'unctuous' approval by the *New Statesman*. Yet when such crimes are reported, they are treated as "atrocity stories".

And better citizens than you or I:
But ever in the cause of the Hyena
They'll take the controversial arena—
A sort of "Rabid Canine Friends Society"
Who go beyond the Deans in slimy piety,
To boost the Anarchist, whose foetid breath
Is perfumed with the carrion worms of death,
Who chooses graveyards for his camps: for rooms
To kennel in the charnels and the tombs:[1]
This Mystic of all negative distortion,
Even the Reds regard as an abortion—
Decadence never stank, till now, it's true,
And Beardsley was a pearl of morning dew,
Since literature has lived divorced from life
As a mad cuckold from a hated wife
In love with Death and still by her rejected
Save only where the brainworm is respected.
Even the Communists get conscience-stricken
To see these moral paralytics sicken
And bump them off by dozens at a time
When they out-charlotade the bounds of crime . . .
Were but our writers to spare moral reasons
To tartuffade their anti-human treasons,
To spare that sickening sweetness and humanity
With which they butter-scotch the base inanity
Scavenging like the bees around the rose
Wherever foul corruption picks its nose!
For here we're not concerned with any Cave-man
The anarchist's the pure and simple Grave-man,
The walking mummy, exiled from his home,
In the sub-real, ten feet beneath the loam,
The sickliest fungus of a rotten culture
Engaged, himself, upon his own sepulture.

Though to their side momentously was rolled
The mountainous advantage of the gold:

[1] Anyone who saw the desecrated cemetery at Huesca where the anarchist artillery was parked, will never forget it. They had set up a bar: and in their spare time were ransacking the coffins for rings, crucifixes, and gold teeth. Shrouds, coffin planks, skulls, legs, and arms littered the ground for a couple of acres.

And worth as much, when minutes were so short
And miles so long, the tankers in the port:
The snorting horsepower of the sea and land,
In cornered petrol, nuzzled to their hand,
By them corralled beyond the millionth ton,
Which we must crease or lazo on the run:
With telegraphs and 'phones, with rails and wires
From town to town conducting their desires,
Of the whole land they had the voice and ears
When we were deaf with blows and blind with tears:
While weak with loss of blood, and numbed with fright,
We saw the rabble, absolute in might,
Loosed from the gaols, armed from the magazines,
Turning the streets to shambles and latrines.
With weeks for Centuries, in killed and burned,
The Roman circuses to life returned,
Trebled themselves, the Cæsars to depose,
And throned the Comrade with the purple nose,
Where cranium measurements became the Crown
And Finger-Prints the seal of all renown,
And the fierce spirochete, with might and main,
The raging dog-star of the human brain,
Knouting the cells, became the ruling Tsar,
To vomit fire and pestilence afar,
While syphilis and alcohol began
The death-dance of Regenerated Man,
And Christians learned, upon a stage more grand,
What bloody Circus was our Native land!
Theirs were the Aegis and the thunderbolts,
That from the towering pylons loose the volts,
Where roost the rookeries of winged words,
And shake them through the sky like migrant birds
Which have the power of panic in their wings
To bear the lies to foreign states and kings:
Out-plaguing Egypt, never hummed the skies
With locusts as the ether now with lies
Nor Lenin's "mightiest arm" more fiercely plied
Its Red vendetta against human pride,
Believed by most: for in its cause to plead
Negligent honour keeps no lawyer fee'd,

And Propaganda ill accords with pride
But barks its head off on the guilty side—
To set the world against us with its votes
Whose only crime was to defend our throats;
Until those towering trees, that leafed with lies,
Began to flower with answers and replies,
Like bees and humming-birds to sip the dew
The churchman and the intellectuals flew,
And never yet were trilled with livelier notes
The Tartuffades of Anglican devotes.
So soon those pylons groaned with heavier fruits
Foreign supplies, and swarms of Red recruits,
That came in such a record-breaking crop
That weight of numbers brought us to a stop,
By avalanches brought upon one knee
And forced to duck each time we shook the tree—
But as Antaeus, when he touched the earth,
From our bent knees our victories have birth,
Down on our knees our fiery strength we stem
And prayer's to us what dynamite to them.
To have the loaded batteries, cells, and wires
Primed for the expert gunnery of liars;
The power, the fleet, the air force, in their hands
Save what in ours had come away in strands—
No pity then when all was in their powers
And round our heads were bombed the reeling towers,
And yet no whining on the part of ours!
To have the keys, rails, centres, and the straits
And be the wardens of our own shut gates,
Through which, as spooks, we had to glide our spoors,
To leak through keyholes, and to fade through doors—
The very straits sharked by the submarine
Were redder than their surfaces were green:
To see the dice so loaded—you'd have said
Dynamics and Geography were Red
To Federate the Lightnings and the Gales
And Bolshevize the Ocean with its Whales—
And then get drunk in proper "comrade" fashion
To find we'd seized the arms and bagged the ration,
Which is their chief excuse and major reason

For being gudgeoned in and out of season,
Who rise red-eyed from rapes and drunk debauches
To find our banners streaming at their porches—
And is the answer to each canting fool
Who deems such drones were ever fit to rule,
And shows the Right hand is the hand of workers
And the shut Left—of parasites and shirkers,
And that Democracy has had its hour
That shoves such sleepy scullions into power,
Which only as a system could be borne
When Christians held barbarity in scorn
And, with the land-myths, nourished with the sod
The voice of peoples was the voice of God.
Ere poisoned by the radio from the sky
And half electrocuted with the lie
The great Majority were numbed to die,
And twilight would have settled on their brains
Had we not come, the riders of the plains,
To fox that Talking Mongoose[1] from the sky,
The gait of living effortless at last
And Meetings now a nightmare of the Past!
The whole of Modern Science and Invention
Went to the Left it seemed by God's intention
And took the Gold lest, where her cause should crumble,
Materialism should have cause to grumble,
The dice were doctored with her own false hand
When in her bout with Faith she staked the land,
And it should prove beyond the least denial,

[1] The Talking Mongoose of the Isle of Man: a rival radio and press
sensation to the late George Steer's famous hoax about Guernica's
being destroyed by aerial bombardment, the most typical and successful
of all these prevarications. He must have known, as we did a week
before, that the total destruction of the City had been expressly ordered
by the Minister of Works Pascual Tomas: on the Radio and in the
Press, his famous utterance was everywhere quoted, "We shall make
veritable Numancies of these cities" (Guernica and Durango). I quote
from *Lucha*, April 21st 1937. "Haremos destas ciudades verdaderos
Numancias." The attempt at total destruction was foiled. That third
of the town which comprised the arms factory was successfully gutted
with dynamite and petrol. The Nationalists saved two-thirds of the
town. Unlike Numancia it had been evacuated. Durango was saved
intact.

In her own language, by her own gross trial,
Beyond appeal, and openly to view,
Which was the least a bumpkin of the two.
And many now would give a sum to hide
What then they wrote in plutocratic pride
Our "penniless adventure" to deride,
When sneering at our lack of arms and cash
They called it, neither foolhardy nor rash,
But "sheer premeditated suicide,"
When on the plains "invincible" was hurled
The Army of the People of the World,
The hoarse blaspheming of the godless horde
Against the Cross and Crescent of the Lord,
The Cross, our Hammer, and the Quarter Moon
Our Sickle, and Hosanna for our tune!
Although in foreign aid by one to four
Outnumbered as preceded months before,
Which on our side was proffered, not entreated
As when to "Workers of the World" they've bleated
Their myriad S.O.S.'s through the skies—
To prove how "Spanish" is their enterprise!
As to the Moors, whom they were first to bribe
With their Autonomy—that swarthy tribe
Whom they invited first, why should we ban
When they proclaim the Brotherhood of Man
When Chinks and Chuckchees pour with might and main
To swell the People's Army on the plain,
How else into our hands chanced these to fall
Five hundred tailless apes from Senegal,
As regulars enlisted one and all?
Azaña's ten pesetas to refuse
And fight for five—the Moors were free to choose
And be called "Mercenaries" as are we
Who in the Legion are content with three,
While Requetés and Falangists fight free—
And only "Patriots" claim the larger fee![1]

[1] There was more Abraham than Lincoln in the famous American brigade to judge from the prisoners; and they fought magnificently. Jews and Arabs are generally at loggerheads. It is of course as arrant antisemitism to object to Arabs fighting in Spain as to Jews, both being Semites.

In all the news of Spain it will be found
The Labels have been stuck the wrong way round—
That Moors should fight for us, small wonder, too,
Since on their side the Reds have got the Jew—
You cannot have your cake and eat it too!
Without Autonomy, without more pay,
They chose with us the clear equestrian way,
That links the herdsmen to the whole world's end
Wherever out of Abel we descend:
Rather to help the rightful heirs of Man
Than rule with sub-men on an equal plan.
Too near in blood the grumble to advance,
As *near* as Senegal is *far* from France
With troops recruited from the tops of trees
From the less agile of the Chimpanzees—
Poor Islam's had no cause for hesitations
Betwixt Democracies and the Dictations,
And well she knows how her victorious aid
By Democratic countries is repaid,
Who bombing their best allies to their shame,
Vainglorious Mussolini dare to blame
For treating his worst enemies the same!
Of Liberty or Freedom they've enough
Who've learned to dread the namby pamby stuff—
Since both have wrung them fiercely by the scruff!
They think of each as of a blood-dripped Ogress
And know there is most headway where least "Progress."
Remembering Russia,[1] in her injured pride
The Moon of Islam sunk their godless tide,
But, joined with Italy, could count far less
Than this huge League of Nations in Distress,
Of whom we've buried more in French alone
Than live Italians can with us be shown.[2]

[1] Ten pesetas was the pay of the Red Militiamen. A few days before the great popular Rising, Azaña on Radio Madrid implored the Moors to join the Reds. As the French use Senegalese to quell riots in France and as the Spanish Republic used them to quell the Asturias rising in '34, republican objection to their use is hypocritical.

[2] This was written after most of the Italians had returned to Italy. The balance between French and Italians was about equal numerically though not as regards fighting strength. 36,000 French were missing in

The scum of Europe into it was poured
And facing there the hydra of the horde,
The fauna of the steppes, the dregs of drains,
From Ainus down to France's quadrumanes,
We multiplied its heads the more we slew
Although like side-show coconuts they flew—
And by Brunete you may see in stacks
Dead bodies climbing on each other's backs
To make a huge paella of the plains,
A dish of rice, with corpses for the grains,
Whom safe intriguing pedants sent to die
And sell their scrawny mutton for a lie,
To perish for an ignominious cause:
Not as our "dead," in rhyme with Cosmic laws,
Who die as queens in childbed, giving birth
To the resurgent order of the earth
In certain victory and faith unshaken
Since first Red Saville with ten men was taken,
When in Red hands lay Spain all crushed and gory
And in our hearts the hazard and the glory!
And "Viva la Muerte" when we cry
That valiant comrade never lets us die,
Whose every death's a splinter of the Cross
Redeeming Victory as theirs reap loss.
Our deaths like towering stones are piled on high
To lift a great cathedral to the sky
And stand in rock, the thunders to defy;
While theirs form dumps of excavated sand
To room its deep foundations in the land,
Their only monument a vacuous hole
And ours a towering temple in the soul:
Theirs the lugubrious dirges in the distance
Where birth-controlled into a false existence
The sons of Onan, in the mists forlorn,
Lament their evil fortune to be born
And through the world unbroken and the same
Would socialize their misery and shame,

'37 from manœuvres, the reason given in the "Chambre de Deputés" being that they were in Spain. As foreign aid, they outclassed the blackshirts completely, so did the "Garibaldis."

Which life rejects with ridicule and scorn.
For as our test, the touchstone of our right,
To sink these new Cromagnons out of sight,
Whose impetus is not to breach the tomb
With souls immortal forging through the gloom,
But hankers back to the prenatal womb—
It was demanded that, against all odds
Imaginable, we should face their Gods
Of Economics, Science, Gold, and Sex,
And, naked, force the yoke upon their necks:
Against the very lightnings of the sky,
The ether volted with one towering Lie,
To prove ourselves reluctantly, though pressed,
With their own arms (which, first, we had to wrest)
By their own standards, and their chosen test,
The fittest for survival and the best:
To force their Evolution into fact
When by that foul inversion we're attacked
And all our clergy into catsmeat hacked:
To illustrate, with deeds, their boasted aim
Which as their sole religion they proclaim
To "liquidate the useless and the lame."
And if we did not do it long before
Say, when Gil Robles held the reins of war,
"Thou shalt not kill" was what we waited for:
The binding ban that cannot be untied
Save by the stronger—that on Suicide:
Since for five months we'd turned the other cheek
And only stalled the Terror by a week.
Never was physical advantage vaunted
As by the Reds: nor penury so taunted:
But soon the stores, the petrol, and machines
Came over to our hands by their own means:
It seems they came to ask us for employment
Since in our hands they found the best enjoyment
For matter loves to leap in lovely acts
As show the rainbows and the cataracts,
Gets tired in the mere positive to live
And likes a jaunt in the superlative,
With valour looping, seeking where the God is,

In training, as it were, for when, set free,
Its elements will form in human bodies
Just as we train in war, cadets to be
For our commissions in the Seraphry—
For it was Sick of the obscene satanics
Of those who make a Gospel of Mechanics,
Tired of its pusillanimous alliance
With those who make Religion out of Science—
And soon the Russian experts showed as boobs
With anything that can't be kept in tubes,
Stamp-tallied, or methodically docketed—
But in this war the prayers of martyrs rocketed,
The powers of Faith were loosened on the air,
And gum and scissors failed to cope with prayer.
Materialists have done far more to shatter,
Than any one, the patient nerve of Matter
Which the most fiery mystics always found
So tame and humble (when they touched the ground)
And showed, as organizers, far more sense
Than these materialists—incompetence,
Since "Wrecking" amongst Matter-sodden races
Has proved the title to the highest places,
Tracking each other's bloodspoor as they slink
One after one, each other's blood to drink,
To bugle round the world from zone to zone
The One Discovery by Science made known—
It's better to bow down to wood and stone
And worship them with human sacrifice
Than worship nothing at this bloodier price
Of millions slain for greater filth and famine;
Since every "Reformation" we examine
That sprung from lack of Christian Resignation
Has plunged the world in deeper desolation:
And "Progress" is another way of trying
To kill an invalid, to stop him dying,
To rid the world of pain on the assumption
That colds are cured by Galloping Consumption.
The Inquisition in six hundred years
Pumped not a thousandth of the blood and tears
As, in some twenty, has the world-reforming,

Free-thinking, Rational, Cathedral-storming
Humanitarian, with his brother love,
To whom Tsarism was a sucking dove
And Hitler was to this degrading sham,
As to a rabid skunk, a snow-white lamb.
The pains of godless scientists[1] and scholars
Have brought us worse than Patagonian squalors,
Saharan Famine, Dust-bowls, creeping drought,
Death in the Spirit and despair without,
And yet to-day the thinkers and the sages
Can patronize the towering middle ages
As being somewhat Bigoted and Narrow—
The sow of Bigotry could never farrow
Until the true freethinker came along
And liberated "Reason" grew so strong,[2]
Intolerance into delirium blazing
And Bigotry the hair of crime upraising—
To justify whatever Inquisition
To such a lust of blood could be physician,
Restoring it to its intended place
As warder and protector of the Race—
They made mere lunacy limp far behind,
And all the bloodiest manias of the mind,
To this of souls, seem innocent and kind:
Till one could wish a death by their own knout
To those who made religions out of doubt
Like rabid bloodhounds maddening men to slaughter
Who blame their hydrophobia on the Water:
Which by its raving could convince a clod
Of the reality and life of God
Whose absence roared so terribly, Whose lack
Could so disfigure, mutilate and hack
(Worse than their victims) those whom it afflicted,
Who seemed, from human lineaments evicted,

[1] This was written before Einstein made us a present of the Atom bomb.

[2] More people have been imprisoned for Liberty, humiliated and tortured for Equality, and slaughtered for Fraternity, in this century than, for any less hypocritical motives, during the whole of the Middle Ages.

To roar and whinny like the ghouls of Hell
Which (if not elsewhere) here was proved as well,
Converting me to seek Him on the spot,
To see that foul Abyss where He was not:
To find no evidence my sense to dim
But to pure Evil was the lack of Him,
Exasperated to a white-hot glow
By the mere consciousness that this was so—
As it proclaimed itself in speech and fact
And by the loathing in each studied act.
And this identity alone sufficed
To drive an open reason straight to Christ,
No longer open then, but signed and sealed,
To side with Nature and to take the field,
For even their machinery rebelled
And as by miracles, our armouries swelled:
Till we could almost pray for what we wanted
And take the answer to the prayer for granted,
And with our Pater nosters and Hail Marys
Were liming Aeroplanes like tame canaries:
They came down singing to the left and right
And on our very doorsteps seemed to light
Because the "Comrades" in their lying raptures
Of many of our towns had billed the Captures,
So swivelling fleets of armoured cars and lorries
Into our arms, with other welcome quarries.
Heaven through our prayers, Hell through their furious lies
From day to day augmented our supplies:
Their "Mightiest Weapon" in their hands had twisted
And in our cause would gaily have enlisted
Had we the least encouragement bestowed.
We needed tanks: as if they knew the road,
They came like bakers' vans to orders booked,
When the fierce sun their crews of Russians cooked
Who have to be like convicts bolted in—
Surrender being their one besetting sin:
And with the Centigrade at sixty-seven
Their brains were baked and yeasted in their leaven,
And what the sun began, the iron heated,
The Fahrenheit and Centigrade completed,

To save us any need of work more fiery,
As they came nosing to our mazed inquiry,
For the good sun, our ally and physician,
Had kept those dread-vans in the best condition,
Which came to us quite of their own volition
To take our orders and obey us better
Than ever to their owners at Brunete.
The Scottish Ambulance, to crown the laugh,
Delivered both medicaments and staff
Its worthless crew of wowsers to deride
And ask for clean employment on our side,
Renouncing Knox for Scotland's former Grace
As it were conscious to be near the place
Where, led by Bruce's Heart, for Christ and Glory,
Her valiant horsemen topped the peaks of story
And sounded through the world's most manly age
The loudest peal in Froissart's tingling page—
To sink to this, by their own pills and clysters
Disowned for base Geneva-bitten twisters,
Kidnapped by their own lorry as it came
To honk for work, with eager lamps aflame,
As though the shade of Bruce had honked its horn
To hold the modern Scotchmen up to scorn!
But best of all, in this Mechanic treason—
Revolting to our side and with such reason!
Was when the wireless spoke in decent Spanish
And bade the Nightmares of the Nation vanish,
When, like a sunbeam through a dungeon leaking,
Came Quiepo's voice from Red Sevilla speaking:
As if the great Quevedo had not died
That lashing tongue its whip of scorpions plied
And round and round the heavens thrashed their lies
In bat-swarms from their belfries in the skies.
Like lovely rain, we heard his valiant shout,
Over a country killed with dust and drought,
And those who else in dudgeon might have died
Now faced the firing squad with laughing pride.
But clearer far, than in its glad revolt,
In its behaviour, Matter proved no dolt,
And that it has opinions of its own—

As any one who's worked in wood and stone
Can tell you: and that of all things that stir it
It is most pervious to the human Spirit
Whose horsepower, though the Bolsheviks decry,
Propels the graveward hearse in which they lie.
Whether it's guns to fire, or bricks to pile,
Matter is always sensitive to style
(Which is the breathing rhythm of the soul)
And shows itself Devout from pole to pole:
In storms and shocks it always looks for order
The waves in uniform, with silver border,
Still fight to keep in equidistant ranks
As we against artillery and tanks:
Happier still to worship than to grovel
It shows in the Cathedral than the hovel,
And there of centuries will take the polish
Requiring tons of Nitre to demolish:
But when democracy begins to soar
To whom the jail, the brothel, and the store,
Stand for the Church, and tries for like proportions
Matter complies with sorrowful distortions.
And rather as a slave than an ally
"Co-operates" to raise them to the sky,
But always uses them for dump or jake
And does not strain to hold them when they shake,
For still the rot and rubbish most abound
Where Freedom has "collectivized" the ground,
While Monuments and Churches still outlast
The strongest forts and castles of the past,
With the Arenas standing side by side
The first cathedrals of our deathless pride:
And still sun-temples and Stonehenges stand
Praising the Solar glories through the land—
Until our scientists so brisk and nimble
Discovered in the Tree a Phallic Symbol
And other Wowser's Voodoo in the thimble,
And by his guts and sex the Charlie linked
To his destruction, to become extinct,
Unfit to suffer, to create, or strive
Where only towering virtue can survive,

And even God must suffer, bleed and die
Lest on our hangdog heads should fall the sky.
For if we want with symbols to be taught
You'll find more Crosses in this world for thought,
Scored in the wrinkles of your skin they are
And your whole body is a shafted spar,
With a man on it, hammered day and night:
But the Good Thief was hammered to the Right
And bore the nails with valour and delight,
Unlike the snarling Comrade on the Left
Whose dole and rights all other thoughts bereft
When he was in the high, Majestic Place,
Outsoaring Cæsar and the Suns of Space!
We see the Priests of Famine, Death, and Loss
United in their hatred of the Cross
And far more rabid in their anti-creed
Than fervent in the causes they would speed
In which they're hydra-headed, only here
Their necks in one great celluloid appear
And in the common halter of defeat,
Where all as in one goitred neck they meet
To make one think the collar and the shame
Are one concentric zero and the same—
To see what are their sole two points of union
Should drive the very devil to communion.
The hatred of the Cross is their Disaster,
Than the great flood, a cataclysm vaster:
Thinking to tear it down, they tore the Sky,
A rain of blood, and lightning from on high,
And the great thunder, headlong and terrific,
When Abel stretched his length to the Pacific
The land a murder, and the wind a cry:—
And hence a War *for* War, to the last breath,
The Sword He came to bring, the Sword of Death!
No "War-to-end-War" (and beget ten more!)
To "fight for Peace," the Babylonian Whore,
The turtle-winged Sow that comes to farrow
Bloodbaths for which the ocean is too narrow:
A war for eagles—not for turtle-doves
Henpecked to bleeding corpses by their loves!

A war for warriors, not for pacifists
Who tear the living womb with gory fists
Who rape, castrate, and torture, and deplore
With lifted hands the very name of War!
And well may they abominate the Sword,
The bared and naked vengeance of the Lord—
And curse the Soldier, him, the human brand,
That came to lop the sacrilegious Hand,
And root the godless vermin from the land:
For wounds are wings for those who know where God is,
Junkers and Fiats are our slaughtered bodies.
It was not we who lead-swung to the Pities,
When half the loveliest of our ancient cities
Were in the clouds rebuilt—if flames could take them
And rushing smoke restore them in the sky,
When rivers were alive—if blood could make them,
Our blood that had not had the time to die!
Since their intention was not, as they've sworn
To finish off the idle and outworn,
But (as we've proved it openly enough)
To exterminate the valiant, strong, and tough—
And by a sudden knifetwist in the scruff!
That the most abject might assume the Seat
And heads be trampled by their dirty feet,
That crime might flourish, sodomy abound,
And Love be crushed forever to the ground:
There as they raped, and sodomised, and lusted,
By their obscene babooneries disgusted,
Indignant Venus played them wicked pranks,
Sending, incognito, into their ranks
The twin *milicianas*, Pox and Clap,
Who operated to such dire mishap,
Dispensing, free, to officers and rankers
Their running sores, and fistulæ, and chancres,
That to their charms more casualties fell
Throughout the war (as captured records tell)[1]

[1] One does not need to go to the captured records to know the
babooneries that went on. In Langdon Davies' *Behind the Barricades in
Spain*, this Red supporter gives an account of how "Free Love" was
enforced on the women, apparently with his approval.

Than to the heavy toll of shot and shell.

Yet all their knowledge could be used to *save*—
Even what they burrowed from the Ape Man's grave
And vulgarized into a murderous creed:
They teach us (as the Anarchists to-day)
The Grave is Sacred, it will search and slay
Its desecrators, and destroy their breed,
A knowledge worth all Huxley's dreary screed.
A far worse vengeance than the Pharaoh took
Came from the Ape Man's miserable spook
Who still with fury chivvies them to-day:
For though they had the live created Adam
Like a Rolls Royce upon the blue MacAdam
Of time, his body like a golden dream,
The stream-lined dolphin of the vital stream—
With Michaelangelo to see that Car win
Like a great Malcolm at its solar wheel,
It roused their abjectness and loosed a Darwin,
Whom any Inquisition would repeal,
And let that bungling workman fit in parts
Of obsolete machines and rusted carts:
And if we have to go to Davey Jones
For our spare parts, among the rocks and stones,
The Aurignac man could spare us better bones,
Heighten our foreheads, and square out the shoulder,
A handsomer progenitor, though older,
Than those with which they bestialize our breed,
Since you could make a theory no bolder,
That we are but Aurignacs gone to seed:
For Capitalistic lore, as Communistic,
Must first of all discredit all that's mystic
To sell the mind and body cheap for slavery
Degrading them by slow hypnosis first,
In which the Modern poets head the knavery
In all the arts of degradation versed,
The coolies and the agents of the Jew
Whose only passion is to gripe the two,
And never let their memory escape
The angry vengeance of a bone-rigged ape—

As if Created Adam but exists
Through kind permission of anatomists,
And life were a condition of the body
Not vice versa, as the merest noddy,
By reasoning, can swiftly ferret out,
Till reason makes him sceptical of doubt.
As great Marconi by sheer instinct knew
Lord of the sightless forces of the blue,
But which the humbler unillumined mind
By obvious comparisons can find—
Unless his brain's been pommified in slices
Or soused in muddy draughts of Cam or Isis—
Simply contrasting both in peace and war
The works of faith with those of Charlie lore—
For see these broken walls arise in prayer
Which they destroyed in impotent despair,
The fountain running where the stream they cut,
The flour-mill turning that for months was shut.
Where "progress" turned the villages to pyres
From new-built hearths a different smoke aspires
And as for fighting, though our ranks were spare,
Behold those mountains of dead Charlies there!
Then tell me Science is the God of War
And not its batman, which we take him for,
Who better answers to our curse and rod
Than to their faith who treat him as a god,
For though we study him with equal skill
It is to rule him, not to serve his will:
For any fool can tell you he had none,
Save for some scient-anarchists who shun
The evident, as blind-worms do the sun.
Without a moral value he remains
A menial still for all his active brains,
And better serves a master for his meals
Who keeps him in his place, and firmly deals,
Than when he rules promoted to the fore—
As Sancho wise in proverbs found before,
Solomon and Aurelius had not more
Wise Apophthegms than thronged that lousy pate
On all affairs of government or state—

And yet poor Sancho had to abdicate.
The same with Science and the same with Art—
Without the horse to which they are the cart
They break away, colliding down the hill
And at each jolt, a posse of Charlies spill,
Whether it be philanthropy or crime,
To be the laughter of succeeding time,
As Haldane came back sneezing from Madrid
And Beaujannec got caught with what he hid.
So Science as a deity of war,
Takes a low rank, with Mithras, Mars, or Thor,
As makeshifts all, for want of something more:
Who though he takes our side, could never father
Giants of the Cabeza and Alcazar,
And shines the best by brave example led
As by our peerless Captain bleeding red,
The living Jupiter, authentic Mars,
Than thunderbolts more terrible his scars,
When on the Cross, victorious and high,
The Eagle Aviator takes the sky
To show us how to conquer and to die:
And prove to all the Devil's routed cattle
The God of Love is still the God of Battle
And when in victory our labours cease,
The Christ of Battles is the Christ of Peace:
And all that is worth-while beneath the sun
By suffering and sacrifice is won:
Not the Hortensia pale of the "Renaissance"
With fleshy angels in polite obeisance
Correctly twining to an easy Cross—
But the wide-winged and wounded Albatross
The tempest-torn, that rides (and bears) the strife
And soars upon the hurricane of life:
The Christ, the Emperor of the *Middle Ages*
Of human dignity, resigned, and brave,
Before the dotage of our bards and sages
Who since this second childhood only rave
The human race from suffering to save
Even at the cost of life; when suffering
Is all we have to conquer to be king

Of more than worlds; but were it once removed,
Lower than dogs we'd live, by life reproved,
Scorned by the angels as effete buffoons
And spat on by the devils as poltroons.
For there's been no "renaissance" up till now
Except for Galathea's croup and prow—
This is the dawn of Psyche mortified,
The spirit, and the martyr, and the bride!
Only by suffering, suffering can be killed
Only by dying life can be fulfilled,
Death slain, and the lie given to the Charlie crew,
Who shouldn't have been born, and say so too!
The Christ of Salamanca teaches this,
The devil-routing Lord of the Abyss
Who, till this time of men resigned and bold,
Ignatius was the last man to behold—
Since then, till now, men fought for greed or lust
To seize the booty or to bite the dust,
But the old world is "braver" than the "new,"
Can use it as its foot-stool or its shoe:
Or when it rots as it's begun to do,
As a sharp knife can cut that Stilton through
Cough though the scientist or squirm the Jew,
Or stink, abjectly dead, the poets too.
That God was never brilliantined or curled
Who out of Chaos saw his battles won,
And gave, like Moscardò, his only Son,
To save the charred Alcazar of the world.
For of all gods, he only breathed our breath
To live the solar myths, and conquer death:
In his last highest creature, as his least,
Fulfilled the law by which they are increased,
And stooping to her sternest law, allied
His nature to our own as to a bride,
In one fierce act of suffering and of strife
From mutual death to wrest immortal life,
For that same principle He died to crown
To life's most humble sources filters down,
And easier in their tiny worlds is seen
Than in our own more complicated scene,

Wherein the miracle's but dimly spied
(Unless that inspiration is our guide)
Which from the glory of His bleeding wings,
Out-soaring Cæsars, paladins, and kings,
Nature reflects into her humblest hive[1]
Where One must die that generations thrive—
And even in our own ejected seed
Creation is the Devil-Darer's deed
Who wins the ovum by his strength and speed,
As in the bee that resurrects the breed,
In death to triumph, over death to drive,
And die of Love, to save the race alive,—
Where One ascends to triumph and to bleed
To form the generation or the Creed,
On whose immortal, onward-rushing wave
He rides superb across the open grave
That gapes to swallow the rejected drones,
And there while they await the final chill,
Like Bloomsburies, perhaps, in envious need
They'll sit and patronize the Victor's deed
Or, as the English poets, stray forlorn
And curse their evil fortune to be born—
The miracle and Fiat to deny
Of which they are the residue flung by,
While through his saints and soldiers runs the spark,
The rose and rapture that defies the dark,
To whose adventure life and death are flame
And both conduct to victory the same,
Since if His soldiers lose the brighter crown
It is for earthly conquest and renown.
And here the warring principles are shown
Betwixt the male and the rejected drone:

[1] It is an English Protestant superstition that anything animals do is good. This was written to pull Gide's leg and to show how naturalistic arguments can be held against Naturalists. Gide justified his vices by those of dogs. "Dogs do it" is Gide's apology. Dogs eat their own vomit, sometimes their litters of puppies, as pigs and rabbits often do. I don't think it means we ought to follow suit. The only animals that practise Gide's vice in wild nature are canine in appearance:—the hyena (often a hermaphrodite) and the baboon, always a sissy till his third year.

The latter would for safety break their necks
Reducing life to comfort, food, and sex:
The former all-accepting soar above
To triumph over death and die for love,
For as the lucky seed, against all odds,
From germ to man, from manhood to the gods
Aspires: a war eternally must redden
Betwixt the solar instinct and the leaden,
Though the advantage be to those who deaden.
Not Cæsar soaring to his lonely tower
Superb in beauty, aquiline in power,
His world-wide circle round the sun can fling
But their dull thoughts, like pellets in his wing,
By treachery must bring him hurtling down
By sacrifice to consecrate and crown,
And so much more when all unarmed they spy
The mightier Cæsar of the earth and sky.
Even from stone his likeness must be razed
Or when upon a living face it's blazed—
As when the good Sotelo fell in gore,
But resurrected on the wings of war
His spirit, with his Master's wounds astream,
Arose his butchered country to redeem—
Such sacrifices consecrate our cause
In serving the divine and earthly laws.
Since on this earth an atheist never trod
All men are either for or anti-God:
Even these anti-Gods depend on Faith
Which if they died would take no kind of scathe,
But if the Faith were dead, doubt would explore
A hollower existence than before,
With no more crumbs to pilfer but instead
A notice up to say "The Baker's Dead":
For all who by negation try to live
Depend on what the positive can give—
And so the parasite who kills his prey
Must feed on his own flesh or fade away.
When Bolshevisms's left upon the hob,
With no one else to murder or to rob,
Then suicide becomes its only job—

Wolves wolfing wolves, bears over-bearing bears,
And Socialism slaughtering its heirs,
Lest mere experience should teach these comics
Some rudiments of life or economics
(Which any simple yokel on his own,
Can settle for himself if left alone),
As now in Russia they seem "taking notice,"
For Stalin's knife is still where Lenin's throat is.
In all affairs of comfort, food, or pelf
The poor materialist defeats himself:
Wherever Bread or Money's the religion
The death of it extends through all the region:
Hyenas, "Blums," Staviskies, pimps and sharks
Have made their Father Christmas out of Marx
And strikes and famines follow grim and stark,
Wherever his goloshes leave their mark—
The bread goes black, lead mingles with the "duro"
To spoor this bleak Messiah of the bureau—
And you may search Madrid or Barcelona
For any sign of Ceres or Pomona:
From his infected presence to the mystics
They fly: but first with his profound statistics
They play the devil, spoiling every plan;
Such is their hatred of the Fallen Man—
But plenty follows still with sumptuous Feast
Earth's triumvirs, her wise men of the East:
The Soldier, and the Prophet and the Priest
Though these are best on fiercest hardship bred
The snow for blanket and the rock for bed—
From them the rosy wine, the silver bread!

Book II

In Spain, where Lenin thought his way was clear,
If anywhere within the human sphere
Then communism should have triumphed here,
For through the land for years it mined and holed
And trawled the gutters with its seines of gold:
What was corruptible in all the land
Was long ago a pawn in Moscow's hand—
And that it was corruptible, was broken
No sooner than its "No" to life was spoken,
For having lost the true and vital track
Of destiny, some bungled ages back,
Which all must lose who lose their sense of sin—
That poison riots and revolves within:
And had it killed us it would still have rolled
In agonies, till it was stark and cold:
(Geneva so, its ward-mate, nearest death
By the worst jerks was galloped out of breath
And did its greatest harm upon its bier,
Throwing the fiercest fits of its career,
From which the world but barely tumbled clear).
To hook it was our final act, though first,
But after that its fury must be nursed,
Though many took for growing strength, its rage
From primary to tertiary stage—
As a grey shark, the "Comrade" of the main,
That, stalling to the horsekick of the cane,
Weaves his great circle, like a trail of milk,
And tons of water, triggered by the silk,
Hang on his fins and turn to watermills
The rooster-combs that tremble in his gills,
Till from the huge compression of his heart
As from a charge of cordite he must part;
His pain the tube, his agony the gun,
His furious projectile leaps the sun,
The traces spiral round him to his head
Boxed by the sinker with its fist of lead,
The cutting Sickle of his tail as vain

As the great ram and Hammer on his brain,
With fins all porcupined, in sidelong share,
He rounds upon a foe that is not there,
Till drowned, his blood with waterbubbles mixed,
By his own speary strength he lies transfixed,
And self-harpooned, self-strangled of his breath,
Is brought to bed of his last orphan, Death—
The fisher hauls his body to the slip,
Around whose bulk the happy children skip,
Bathers feel warmer round the arms and thighs,
Only the intellectual droops his eyes
And his subscription to the papers sends
For the protection of "Our Scaly Friends."
With our right hand and dominating skill
We sense the tactics of that frantic will,
And round the great stockade with whip and line
Can play the epileptics of his spine,
Confining here, exasperating there,
We play him off against his own despair,
More dangerous as he draws near his end
And the great pangs their spinal voltage send;
Switching the current as we haul or slack
Our hand convulses each renewed attack,
The great buckjumping throes that rend his back,
As still his failing spirit strives to straddle
The jerks and jolts that jump it from the saddle,
While through his vertebrae like rattled stones,
The marrow, like an injured snake of bones,
Rears to each fierce parabola of pain
That rockets through their dislocated chain,
Till, like a boa constrictor, thwarted Sin
Recoils with havoc on the soul within.
Where others see in each return to strife
A new vitality or lease of life—
We know his violence and his swiftening breath
Momentously are magnetized by Death
Where Gravity, engrafted with the bone,
Exerts, as in the headlong fall of stone,
The Will of the Earth-Mother, linked with ours,
The force that tests, the vengeance that devours,

Whose upward-climbing force, with ours aspires
To throw down all of which the Cosmos tires,
A weight of crushing guilt, it loads the foe,
But of our white resilience strings the bow,
To keep us anchored till our task be done
Lest we should rise and vanish in the sun,
For these great forces come the world to wake
Spurn at the ground with every stride we take,
And the earth's reigning at our upward verve,
With singing line, as to a kite will serve;
Through it we weigh the prize of every limb,
Queued for enlistment in the seraphim:
Its gentle thorn still conscious in our skin
To goad the working chrysalis within,
It keeps us still in love with earthly things
Lest yet we take our plumeless arms for wings
Before their scarlet feathers have been grown
And the deep wounds have quilled them to the bone.
But here we must be ballasted awhile
Till we remind the valleys of their style,
The ancient rhythm broken to restore
And teach the corn to rustle forth once more,
To wake from her enchantments and despair
The sleeping princess with the yellow hair
And fence her safety with our ridge of steel
That she may ride at our advancing heel,
Once more full-skirted with her waving plume
Her empire of the prairies to resume,
While the red poppies at her call aspire
With fangs of gold, and baying scent and fire,
Close at our stirrups race with lolling tongue
Like hounds to hunting when the world was young
To bark the "comrade" up the nearest tree,
The lewd baboon that would not let her be—
For we must save creation for our sons
However much against the grain it runs
To hunt that base Neanderthal with guns,
For only on the frontiers of the Styx
Is room for him whose blood can no more mix
With ours than lukewarm gravy can with fire,

Who weighs his grudging sweat against his hire
When sacrifice is what the gods require;
And those in whom the solar glory strives
Like willing horses thrash and flog their lives
Until they drop; for to a soul of flame
All raptures beside sacrifice seem tame,
And we must pay, long overdue, the debt
Our enemies have shirked, of Adam's sweat,
Both for themselves and us, and so continue
The lease we only hold with straining sinew,
Which "rights" and "freedom" would fob off and shirk,
But we'll accept, though treble be the work,
Till over the corroded, cratered plain
The coloured harvest spreads its ruddy stain
And through the land expands its belt of gold
Just as the young moon swallows up the old;
For as the new moon eats the old with fire
Whose blackness is the coal of its desire,
So their black chaos is but welcome fuel
And phoenix-tinder to this fierce renewal
That from such carbon can hydrate the jewel:
Till from the clear shield of the land will scale
The blackened cinder of that injured nail
For the new horn digests the blackened crust
That shrivels, of itself, from self-disgust,
Renounced by those same Marañons and Gassets
That gnawed and blackened first its pearly facets,
Which first they irritated and infected
But then with valiant honesty, rejected,
But which our health unsqueamishly devours
As valiant roots turn rubbish into flowers.
Our own clean hands accept the filth and dirt,
Off the green wound we peel the plastered shirt,
Wash the live ulcer, set the splintered bone,
And tend the sores as if they were our own,
Remembering offal was the food of saints
From which their lips could kiss the evil taints,
While the lewd kisser of the godless thug
Will turn good bread to weevils in his mug:
While spuds—to us, the magnates of the soil,

The alluvial nuggets of our sweat and toil—
Grilled as with frosts, reward his chilling spade
Thrice-honed upon the Minus-centigrade,
With no more relish than if with his hoe
He had sliced off his gnarled and grimy toe,
Whose limping toil provides (for yams and onions)
Kibes of the soil, and vegetable bunions,
Whose price and quality their journals paint
With lamer diatribe and splayed complaint:
But which, were they the all we had to sup with,
We could give thanks for, let alone put up with,
Since the bright Spain, the Spain we represent,
Digests their Spain, and with devout content
Says grace for every bunioned foot of land
That limps, so painful, to her open hand,
Pardons the filth and grime, accepts the stain,
And wipes it with her own bright locks of grain.
Less work, more comfort, and increasing dole,
Inspire the negative and graveward soul,
And from such grudging niggardness will hatch
As drab conditions, with complaints to match,
But those who thank their sires that they were born
And with the roosters praise the darkest morn,
Who ask no dole, who make their sport of loss,
And for their sofa clamour for a Cross,
Crying for gulfs to match against their might
And darknesses to exercise their light,—
Spirits of power and valour and delight
Who know that danger, suffering, and pain
The most of living ecstasy contain,
Thence to be wrestled for with might and main,
As purest radium from the hardest rocks
And proudest victories from the fiercest shocks—
When such as these upon the earth prevail
Her sister planets, turning as they sail,
See a strange glory on earth's lighted face
To compensate the sorrow and disgrace
With which she blushes for that darker strain
And bears the bloody Charlotades of Cain.
And so must Spain to passing stars appear

Two-thirds illumed as in the lunar sphere
And all the rest besmeared with greed and lust,
But there a scythe of light the darkness reaping
And there a Sword with dented edges sweeping:
And often have I blest her humble dust
Sure of the sacred treasure in its keeping,
That holy, holy, holy was the rust
Wherein those twin Excaliburs were sleeping.

Remembering Lenin and his "Powerful Weapon"
You'll find far less Banana peel to step on,
Invert their victories, transpose their labels,
And on his abject ruse you'll turn the tables,
As here their boasted mission turns our own
To purge the country of the Moneyed Drone
And theirs the role they had prescribed for us
To stew in their own juice and raise a fuss,
For though with lies your hearing they belabour
Theirs is the Capital as ours the Labour:
They are the workless plutocrats, content
To sink their harvests fifty-five per cent,
And raise their prices to such eagle height
That profiteering fainted at the sight,
With them the deepest marks suggesting ploughs
Are furrows in their corrugated cows,
And, as their farming had gone worse to seed,
The fields consuming what the beasts should feed,
The windmills gone on strike, or, tick for tock,
Losing a marathon to the village clock:
But look at ours that with the Junkers race
And spill in flour what they devour in space
Whose sails invisible, with slumbrous tune,
Are scarce a blur upon the rising moon:
As for our crops—with such terrific might
The warrior scythe was never seen to fight!
On land, we win a seafight with our plough
Who shares to victory with her cruiser prow,
Of that famed cavalry to dim the feat
That riding on the ocean took a fleet,
Whose furrow heaving surges in the loam

Outstrips the snorting bowsprits of the foam,
Since on dry land her naval fight was hurled
Against the fleets and breadships of the world,
To raise more corn and lay more surplus by
Than the Red horde "collectivized" to die
And more to feed them as we forge along,
In war more valiant, as in work more strong,
Than they with all their treasuries could purchase
Or, pity-mongering, cadge from foreign churches,
Though churches easier than forts they'll scathe
And sacrilege is their sole act of faith!
Theirs but the promises of what we bring
Who all their weight on Propaganda fling,
Wasting more steam on meeting and debate
Than we reserve in silence to create,
For "propaganda" rounds off all their scope
Though our Religion they proscribed as "dope"
Which never yet unfitted men for battle
Or caused them to neglect the crops and cattle
Like that cheap Vodka of the intellect
Which never save as poison took effect,
Like hemp-smoke to confound their acts with words
And breeding lice for rearing flocks and herds—
As in new-rescued lands we can determine
Their live-stock is confined to rats and vermin:
Prize cattle they can make of bugs and fleas
As of defeats their famous victories:
For Propaganda (Mystics of the Lie)
Becomes their Universe, their Earth and Sky,
Until their bluff, invented to deceive,
They are the only gudgeons to believe.
And where in Agricultural Reform
Were lists and figures ever seen to swarm
As there, devouring acres of good paper,
Their cyphers and statistics whirl and caper,
Like the mosquitos of their fevered area
With plagues of economical malaria,
Like stings their soaring prices come to fix,
Till Life's a skeleton of rattling sticks
That jitters with delirium by the Styx—

Which multiplies the bureaucrats and clerks,
As fire with fire, to drive out Marx with Marx
Till all's a chaos, remedy and itch
Confounded and involved to such a pitch,
Except to argue wildly which is which
There's nothing, save to thieve while there's a chance
And rent one's future domicile in France.
For economics shun their laboured course,
But serve us out of habit like a horse,
To prove the economics of the camp
Worth all the sweated oil of Marx's lamp,
One Quartermaster, come to feeding cities,
Worth fifty paid professors on Committees
One Cantinera, come to feeding villages,
Worth all the world of Vladimirs and Ilytches!
And honesty can save more time and pains
Than all the theories of Maynard Keynes,
Which, old and humble, like Aladdin's lamp,
Yet feeds the city and sustains the camp,
And as Spain welcomes home her wandered half,
Slays for the prodigal the fatted calf.
While scores of paid professors on their Boards
Have emptied golden cities of their hoards,
To prove without a further waste of breath
That Bolshevism means decay and death
And like the Arian heresy of old
That thus its final paralytics rolled
Four hundred years after its birth was told,
Is but the Reformation come to roost
Four hundred years after its rage was loosed—
Its highest prophets in their windy pride
Anachronized by corporals on our side
Where Cuesta's simple land-laws are applied,
Torpedoeing the Talmud-heavy bulk
Of Marx's *Capital*, whose sodden hulk
(The Apocalypse of hate-hysteric toil)
Rainbows the wave with tons of midnight oil,
Meaningless hieroglyphics, whose oily hues
Enough to brilliantine the world of Jews,
Or (as we've seen) to set the world on fire,—

Exploded thus, and spilled upon its ire,
Can still the Storm, and make the waves expire.
For still where Marx's influence is least,
Red fields with vestiges of grass are fleeced,
But where his lore we trample and oppose
Reviving Nature thanks us with the rose
And the live earth recovers from his blows—
This fat Cabestro of the starving kine
Had brought old Pharaoh's nightmare into line,
But we supplied the answer to his dream
And drove along the heifers full of cream
With horns of plenty dropping oil and wine!
As Marx the land, so Freud to blast the mind
These creeping desert-makers were designed—
The one by famine to subdue our stomachs,
The one by formulas the mind to flummox,
And both to blast our sense of bad and good
Reducing life to terms of sex and food,
And give us over to their grasping kind
As footballs to be kicked about behind:
But their great error was to sap the breeds
That were to soldier for their ghastly creeds,—
The Russian, now a slave to doubt and fear,
Whether on high his aeroplanes appear
Or when aground, so hesitant to dare,
They lock him in his tank to keep him there:
The Marxian stomach and the Freudian will
That both of death anticipate the chill,
Are both anachronized, at one sole toss,
By those who drain their valour from the Cross.
Frustration is their only sense and aim,
Whose quarrel comes from wishing ours the same,
Their roots of life perverted at their source
And life aborted of its sacred force,
Comparing to our outfit as the tinned
To the live tunny, rainbowed, tailed, and finned,
With solar turbine functioning within
That swirls the nacreous glories on his skin;
And in Red leaders as they plunge and fail
The Freudian virus shows its ghastly trail

Everywhere thwarted and out-soldiered by
The magnanimity they most deny:
For in their deepest project we observe
That hesitation syncopates the nerve,
The tic, the hand's involuntary stammer,
That intercepts the Sickle and the Hammer;
As if the Actual torried them like cows
And passed the Obvious by their angry brows,
The ready-made intelligence is caught
By its own horns of formulated thought,
Which can be gauged and tallied in advance
So foreign to contingency and chance.
They cannot launch the act with the decision,
Armed with a prayer or lighted with a vision,
And vanquished by the forces they decry,
For want of them alone are doomed to die,
For Spirit is the motor fuel of matter
At which they push with such a heaving clatter
And the best "Shell" that was invented yet
Runs from the Cross in living blood and sweat
For power and kilometres to the litre,
Shown here, the nonpareil and record-beater,
The essential oil and attar of all Worth
That drives the thundering turbines of the Earth—
The sovereign Serum, bred in Jewish veins
From Jewish poison, that with mortal pains
The Good Physician suffered to procure,
Against the Devil's fangs to make us sure,
And bore both human flesh and fiendish hate
To furnish that Celestial Mithridate,
Whose vaccination signed upon our heads
Immunes us from the weakness of the Reds,
In whom the poison, though it quick their pulse,
In the long run, will stifle and convulse,
As we have seen with Moscow and Geneva,
Reduced to impotence by the same fever.
For naught's *inevitable* that they do,
In elemental splendour breaking through:
Between the will, the purpose, and the Act,
The interim, as by a cough, is hacked—

No final lyric springs to life intact
Or epic surge with suds of thunder backed:
They get the backwash when the wave has gone
And inspiration would have shouted "On!"
Nor in their homes have they such tales to tell
(If homes survive in that back-street of Hell)
As when Red Seville to Quiepo fell:
No tower of tragedy, Cabeza-crowned,
Head in the stars, and roots in sacred ground.
For them the Lie, false Lenin's "powerful arm,"
For us the living Myth, that grows in charm,
Victory's rainbow! sweetly to inform
The thunder of this harvest-bearing storm,
A smile of beauty on the face of power,
The kestrel moored beside the sailing tower,
The star-beam anchored on the rushing spate,
The flower upon the prison's stony gate,
The sweet guitar that sings in the front line,
The dusty riders' cup of evening wine,—
The thymy myth that with its incense blooms
The mountains and their garrison of tombs,
One with the Race it grew from and sustains,
Drawn from the Epic lava of her veins
To blossom in the thunder-torn moraines,
That from no crabbed empiric springs uncouth
But clings upon the naked crag of truth
To scent the hills with everlasting youth.
And well the Modern Consciousness may storm
Anachronized in all it can perform
And mad with panic, as it reels to stage
The furious aurora of an age
Where all that's Groupy, Left, or Meetingoid
Must go the chainpulled way of Marx and Freud,
While Spain repudiates the breed that barters
And owns the sway of heroes, saints, and martyrs,
Into a thousand useless splinters stunning
The old Régime of Cowardice and Cunning,
But for those souls reserving her delight
Who risk and suffer most to keep her white,
To whose strong arms her radiant charms belong

Which creeping wowsers coveted too long,
With fiery challenges to try and test
The devil-darers that she loves the best,
When only Miracles are worth belief
And Faith has risen to the World's Relief—
That Grand Cathedral, half to ruins turned,
Which Reds and Saxons would have sacked and burned
Which proves that it was for a temple planned
For were it not they'd leave it, like their Land,
To choke with weeds, or like their towns neglect
With bars and brothels festering unchecked:
Not as a Sacred Temple to be wrecked
To look upon it as their lawful prize,
To soil, to plunder, to "collectivize",
To trample on the Miracle it shrines
And run it on co-operative lines.
For once they've made their Market of a Church
They'll leave the population in the lurch,
To rot and starve as in their part of Spain
Where grass forgets to grow and clouds to rain.
Were not the Universe of worship vocal
Their mischief would be leisurely and local,
Not aimed to wreck the whole revolving sphere,
But shot about at random, there and here,
Wherever spires or churches rang their bells
Or cities didn't look like third-rate Hells.
No imbecility they'll find too odd
To illustrate their disbelief in God
And incredulity has made such dupes
With bigots and fanatics for its troops,
That in a world where they're allowed to reign,
Quijote's now the only person sane,
Whose valour has anachronized the clock,
The world-revolving mill that grinds our doom,
And rides the Age like his own spavined crock
Over a gulf which else had been its tomb:
While clocks like windmills droop their broken arms,
He rides through centuries as once through farms,
And like a great round belly in his rear,
The modern world with cautions and alarms

Yells out to him; but cannot make him hear:
While Lenin's gibbering ghost beholds with awe
The outworn Creed which he esteemed as straw
Anachronize the theories he built on
And cleave his iron universe like Stilton,
Till "save the little children" he must roar
Who always scorned hypocrisy before
And half the race to slaughter would not stop
To turn the world into a third-rate shop.
But he rides on illumed with one idea,
"The Fairest of them all is Dulcinea"!
To shout his message to the end of time
The cry that's worth the deathless flowers of rhyme,
Which Judgement's furious Dawn will smile to hear—
To prove his faith, abolishing divorce,
He rides upon his tank-destroying horse
High on the precipice of Faith to prance
With Charlie, like a cockroach, on his lance!
While from our faith such miracles result
The unbelieving bigots to insult,
Whose failures just as obviously obtain
From lack of it, as fevers from a drain,
We move the mountains like ecstatic things
With trees for feathers, forests for their wings,
Sure as the storks in their returning gyre,
Through seas of smoke and hurricanes of fire
Back to the sacred Spain of their desire:
The great sierra with its cloudy mane
Returning like a Trans-Siberian train
With towns for trucks, with exiles and survivors
For freight, and laughing giants for the drivers,
From regions lost in Scandinavian night
Through the Red Seas of Horror and Affright
Like Israel from Egypt, when that Nation
Was pregnant still with the whole world's salvation,
And on its brows the diadem still pearled
Of Adam's sweat, the mandate of the world,
Before they left their heritage seraphic
In usury and drugs to make their traffic,
Or Freuds and Marxes, priests of desolation,

To spread their plagues of famine and damnation,
Death to the soul and Hunger to the land,
The slow paralysis of heart and hand.
But that we move the mountains who'll deny
That's seen us lift them with us to the sky,
For time Eternal jilting narrow Space
Where there's more room with seraphim to race,
With Constellations proudly changing guard
Cabezas and Alcazars to be starred,
That took the sun for their refulgent tyre
And rolled to glory on the wheels of fire
Elija-like, with thunders at the yoke,
While in their wake Vesuvius seemed to smoke
And the great flames released their curling manes
With winged Victory to shake the reins,
Our peerless Nike and Meridian Star
Of all the Seas, the Virgen del Pilar!
While in the streets like phœnixes aspire
The living martyrs with their wings of fire,
And he last eve who stopped you for a light,
Has blazed away to glory in a night,
By amorous fury, as he died of love,
Borne skyward as an eagle bears a dove
But left his friends the valour to consume
The raging fire, the longing for its plume,
The supernatural contempt of doom,
The spirit, in its close corral confined,
That chafes and whinnies to be left behind
And hear its comrade snorting up the wind,
While round Toledo's foetid heaps of stone
For some brief hours about the streets was blown
The scent of roses that were never grown.
Proudly they let the whole world's cables slip:
But first to launch them on their fearful trip,
Their pilots through the thunder of the fray,
With iron valour vascoing their ship,
The Carmelites rose up to show the way:
For martyrdom their eagle spirits burned
As fierce as angry captains for the fight—
In these charred cells where Victory was learned

As others study medicine or law.
In *this* Eusebio prayed whom last I saw—
His flesh already flame, his blood its light—
Questing the fire as fire would seek the straw.
On that dark night, too dark to say "goodnight,"
When what was gentlest in the shaken hand
Cut like a sword—how could I understand
My friends in their true mastery and height?
Or guess at half the fury of delight
That armed these Titans to belittle Death
And made my life, so dear to me that night,
Seem suddenly not worth the waste of breath?
Till those who came to do the deed of spite
Seemed helpless sheep; and these the tigers cruel
Who leapt on their own flesh to rend and tire,
And of their agony consumed the fire
As ruthlessly as fire consumes the fuel.
Prayer was their work (as work's the prayer of slaves)
Whom such an iron servitude made free
Of any purpose but to burn, and Be
That Life, for which our own are yawning graves.
For in our Flash of knowledge, when it lords
A woman's eyes, or glories in the fight,
We only know a shadow of their might
Who with their wounds were out to conquer swords;
Their pardon slew the steel that set them free:
More ample for their captive than the sea,
Each of them caged in his forgiving breast
The bloodshot frenzy of a mob possessed
And hushed it to the whisper of a tree.
So bright they sunned it from their new-found Day
Into the frantic and blaspheming will
Of those who came to raven on the kill,
They knew the eternal Presence of their Prey
And that it was themselves they'd come to slay;
Then from the place they slunk in guilt away;
For These were first to catch the sacred fire
That winged the Phoenix city from her pyre
And made the might of Resurrected Spain
More terrible for every martyr slain

Than in the living impact of her ire.
But of what followed, how shall it be written?
My coward's pen over this thing would gloss
And still my fancy like a nervous kitten
Is clawing at the skein of Atropos—
Cut off from the Alcazar as we lay
With nothing save to listen and to pray,
To listen and to start at fancied sounds
While the Infernal searchers went their rounds,
And life, a fly upon a rum-glass rim
Was subject to the vilest drunkard's whim,
While Death, that kind old wowser with a scythe,
That bearded skeleton with hairless poll,
Seemed but a Lansbury, cheerful and blithe,
A grand old Father Christmas of the soul,
Warm-hearted, benevolent, and kind,
Pickwick in character, Attlee in mind,
In podgy comfort Canterbury's Dean—
Compared to *him* we later heard and saw
To *him* we scented in the Night obscene,
The red hyena, when the rabid froth
In stalactites was drooling from his jaw:
And heard the flesh of women torn like cloth
By female claws: and high above their screams,
Like horrors towering over madmen's dreams
To set the coldest analysts acreep,
The chuckle, and the cackle, and the laughter,
With which that shrill hyena chilled the steep
Crooning their eyeless agonies to sleep—
Most unbelievable and gloating rumour,
Abomination flawless and profound,
Loathing turned joy, as if some fearful tumour
Could find expression in the realm of sound:
Or be translated by a rabid hound,
With hoary mane erect and foetid breath,
Into a cry whose echo in the gloom
Would jog with fear the very bones of death
And bristle up the grass upon the tomb:
For even Hell its huge portcullis slammed
Against the sound, as if it had not known

There is a Region nether to its own
And much to say for merely being Damned!
Than one such night as those of which I tell
I'd sooner have five years of Teruel:
To their suspense the air-raids seemed too brief
Instead of terror, bringing us relief . . .
For there was little difference in one's lot
Whether set free, or whether to be shot,
For freed, it was the gauntlet of the streets,
To lurk in jakes and infamous retreats,
Nearing our quarters with increasing dread—
And some to find our families were dead:
Then without arms, only to have your knife
With which to free your children or your wife
Should the she-werewolves hit upon your spoor
Or bad luck steer them shrieking to your door.
There where we saw the Marist brothers fall
And in their smoking blood upon the wall
"So kills the Cheka" grimy fingers scrawl:
And when they held their rifles to my chest
To save my bacon with a queasy jest,
To take with gratitude their rifle-butts—
My face a pulp, that it might save my guts,
Then when the bloody searchers came in force
How glad to sacrifice my finest horse
Whom in the bull-ring they had known before
Risking his life to feed their Comedor,[1]
And whom those hands that led him forth to die
With thunderclaps had lauded to the sky—
For charity suggests some nobler force
And must be punished—even in a horse!
Then, in the stolen corpse-lorry, the flight
Along the mesa at the fall of night—
The black gore scattered over with loose shingle
While over it the sapphire sparks atingle,
Buzzed, hummed, and trumpeted as if to bring
The judgement of Beelzebub their King;

[1] Bullfights were held in aid of the free public eating-house, or
Comedor de Caridad. In these shows the most famous matadors and
rejoneadores worked free of charge.

That stinking lorry, in my sleep it rides,
The skull and crossbones painted on its sides,
Bounding along the track of broken stones
Like a great skeleton with clanking bones,
While our own friends in ignorant farewell
Followed its progress with a random shell.
Two towers had fallen of those deathless four
That steeper into fame than Andes soar
To dare the loftiest mountaineers of song
(For all but seraphs else would do them wrong)
And to that immortality aspire
Where only the Cabeza[1] holds her spire.
Like foothills to their steep volcanic cones
Valhalla and Olympus sloping lay
And, looking upright, trembled to survey
Those awful craters vomiting their stones
While overhead (not Chimborazo's cloud
More dense and black when thundering aloud)
The leagues of slow bitumen darkly trawled,
And underneath the earthquake nearer crept
By which the hill from its own belly leapt
But left one brood of eagles unappalled;
And though with huge moraines it tore the crest,
And striking here, through endless time was heard,
Broke not the Watch of that Imperial Bird
That on the peak of valour builds his nest:
Of those who saw the hurricane of ire
That rocked the condor on his nest of fire,
None ever guessed that dawn's retarded thrill
With his red eye would find him waking still.
For to the Cordillera they were born
Where courage caps the perils as in scorn
With such a high serenity of snow
That nothing thence but living force can flow:

[1] The Hermitage of Santa Maria de la Cabeza held out for nine months
in the middle of Red Territory. It is probably the world's record considering how few the defenders were. The author was there and back
with messages in 1939 and is still in touch with the only survivor,
Captain Rueda, and the orderly of Capt. Cortes, whose lives were
spared by the 16th battalion of the French International Tank Brigade,
when they were picked up unconscious. The rest were massacred.

Mere valour so surpasses strength and skill,
And Faith so high above our powers must be,
That even when they melt, that tiny rill
Can hurl a thousand valleys to the sea;
For when that huge percussion hit the sun,
And vandals to the eyrie would have won,
So fierce an avalanche upon them fell
Before they knew, their spirits barked in hell.

There while our lorry like a drunken boat
Rocked forwards on the shadowy waves afloat,
The mesa seemed an ocean darkly-burning,
With such a ghostly aura glowed the gloom
As the broad sun to ashes slowly turning
Now to that other torch resigned its room,
That, like a fallen comet, redly bleeding,
Aurora Borealis waving doom,
Or far volcano from a ship receding
From sunken craters fanned its raging plume,
Which spectral through the black, revolving thunder
Forked out, as in its own defiance flung,
And swifter flying as the day went under,
In fierce contortion spiralling its tongue,
In deathless colours on the night unrolled
The scarlet streamers and the stripe of gold!
Yet who that saw its loveliness unfurled
Guessed it the Dawn of Europe: or its wonder
That which should daze the unbelieving world,
And of the Reds of every age and clime
Infuriate the glands of poisoned slime,[1]
To go through history like its Master's face
The target of the soul-destroying race
Blazing more proudly for the pelted grime,
The Glory and Anathema of Time,
Whose memory their thwarted rage will whet
Around its haunting, dreaded parapet,
To keep them firing and blaspheming yet!

[1] A reference to Koestler's and Ilya Ehrenburg's phoney accounts
of the Alcazar, both of whom suppress the account of the blackmailing
of Colonel Moscardó by threatening to kill his child if he did not
surrender, which, of course, they did.

How alien seemed the mesa then and strange
The contours of the well-beloved Range
That home from Talavera o'er the plain
Would trot beside us in its cloudy mane,
That sunlit plain where, never looking back,
(Arré, Caballo!) with resounding crack,
My hand a pistol-shot upon her croup
I loved to feel my bronca loop the loop
While my great dog would thunder forth his mirth
To see the mountains underneath my girth—
That dog (the wolves of Gredos knew him well)
Could wolf the leavings of a whole Hotel,
But now a wolf to his own nature freed
Perhaps on human carrion may feed
And what if, wounded in the mire and stench,
What if one night . . . deserted in the trench . . . ?
I have seen humans under this Red Curse
From things far higher tumble to far worse!
Then little did we hope again to own
That plain where there was not a rounded stone
But we could call a pillow of our own,
Where late into the night the moon and stars
Would tango to the lilt of our guitars:
Where in the noon, the roller on the wire
Would strum the sunbeam, as a hand the lyre,
And if I looked away, with emerald flare
Would change into a bee-eater as fair,
Where finer films the sunlight would confound
And fling a shadow as she cruised around
Like a green lamp reflected on the ground.
Fleeing the land, it was with that dismay
And ache of heart, as when we heard to-day
The "Baleares" foundered in the spray,
Or when the sudden treachery befell
The yet unhumbled towers of Teruel:
Or when at length Saint Mary of the Head[1]

[1] See note p. 195. It is to the credit of the 16th Tank battalion of the
French International Brigade that when the Spanish Reds were slaughtering all the wounded, including the immortal Captain Cortés, the
former saved two or three of these heroes.

The seven-times Alcazar, bleeding red,
After nine months was battered to the ground
Where forty living skeletons were found,
Whose fame as great in tragedy shall shine
As in the roll of victories divine—
Thine, Oviedo: and, Toledo, thine!
But these are tests of the Eternal Rigour
To prove the inward temper of our vigour
That we may win deserving our desire:
They pull us backward as a hand the trigger
To loose the grim compression of our fire,
And for each backward jerk of us, the bigger
Has proved the fierce projectile of our ire:
And never more so than when Mola brave
Or good Sanjurjo hurtled to their grave.
But through the burning country as we passed
Our first disaster seemed to be our last,
Unwelded then by those recurring shocks
Resisting which has turned us into rocks,
Who win more firmness from a thunder-stroke
Than Reds from their few victories can choke:—
For well we knew the harvest would be wrecked,
The cattle decimated by neglect:
The scythe and hammer painted on the wall
Foretold the workless times that should befall,
The skull and crossbones charcoaled here and there
Were auguries of famine and despair,
Where villages already had been turned
To offal-heaps, their churches sacked or burned,
And some to stables, some to brothels turned,
Where the confessionals, as oft we find,
To rites of contraception are resigned—
For things of faith completely to destroy
Their mystic love of sacrilege would cloy,
And still, as the devoutest nuns that live,
They feed on what religion has to give.
Picture the "Godless League" without a god
As music for their sheeny Eistedfodd!
Both atheists and godlessness would out
Had they no God to chew the fat about;

Even the Fiend, to reinforce his sprite,
And get the courage for his daily fight,
Though backwards, says his rosary every night!
And what if Garcia Lorca died for this
Caught bending over that forlorn Abyss
For some mephitic whim his soul that spliced,
As once he boasted, with the Antichrist?
This weary Faustian hunger for the void
An age of intellectuals has destroyed;
In him another Marsyas sang and died,
The victim of the God that he defied.[1]
It was his fate with his own age to die—
That of the fevered sin and languid eye,
And let the new-fledged eagle take the sky,
Whose plumes, the virtues that they found so pale,
Are light and thunder on the roaring gale
Of battle, and have many times repaid
The genius lost in him for Spain betrayed.
For One (whose Absence fills the land entire
With one mad love to emulate his fire)
At the same moment, to the firing squad
Spurning his body, launched his soul to God,
Whose epic line (no flourish of the pen)
Was life and rapture, and whose words were men
And though he died ere it was well begun
Rolls flaming onwards to the rising sun:
For in young Primo's grave his slayers stowed
One fire-brand safe, a whole *mine* to explode,

[1] The amazing amount of paper wasted over this almost unique stain
on Nationalist arms is typical of the Anglo-Saxon Press. When the
Nationalists entered Granada the unbelievable babooneries perpetrated
by the Reds made them trigger-happy as they rounded up and shot all
corrupters of children, known perverts and sexual cranks. A natural
reaction, considering that the week before the Reds had slaughtered and
tortured anyone who was under suspicion of any sort of decency at all.
Maeztu, Calvo Sotelo, Munoz Seca, Padre Eusebio (about to be canon-
ised) and Antonio Primo de Rivera were all killed not for their vices
but for their virtues. They were intellectuals on a higher scale, and died
better than the cowardly Lorca. If the author of this poem, a better
poet than Lorca, so Borges the leading S. American critic points out,
had not been resourceful, he would have died, like Lorca, but at the
hands of the Reds.

And seldom such a triumph (since the Cross)
Has glorified a single human loss:
Whose phoenix blood in generous libation
With fiery zest rejuvenates the nation—
Not like the Reds to seek in "reformation"
A safe escape from suffering or care:
But eager the impossible to dare
Seeking what fort of terror or despair
Can hold its own to Sacrifice or Prayer.
For Victor of the Iron was the corse
When servile Death led forth his winged horse,
And, like a serf, the bridle held to him
As to some Captain in the Seraphim:
While that young Hercules, leaving the ground
He scarcely ever touched, his saddle found
Firm in a Nation's mind, in its strong hand
A stirrup swung where Victory might stand,
And for his charger—cloud-careering Spain
With hide of golden corn and snowy mane,
Tornadoeing in glory through the sky,
In steep sierras caracoling high,
Or in low foothills trotting smooth and fair,
Beneath his sky-blue shirt of morning air
Braided with scarlet arrows by the Sun,
A "Falangist" himself, if there is one!
Punctual at dawn to rise, at eve to set,
And leave the fields ambrosial with his sweat,
And happy now a comrade to embrace
As solar to the land as he to Space,
To whom, as due as to himself, the bread,
Through willing labours, sways its golden head
As never where the countryside is Red;
To whom as due, the storks return this Spring
And homecome swallows in the rafters sing
Secure from last year's dynamiting pest,
The broken eggs, and dislocated nest;
And while these two their bright meridian reach
And pass upon their way with solar speech,
The valiant sun, in little things polite,
To our brave comrade offering a light,

Out of the lovely horses that they drive,
His own appears the grandest of the five—
Heroic steed, of Pantagruelian feats!
Whose footfalls are the shattering defeats
That fall like thunder on the godless scum
And shake the Kremlin with the wrath to come:
Whose hoofbeats are the conquered kilometres
That rhyme along the road in lovely metres,
And all the way from Portugal to France
From victory to victory advance,
Ringing beneath him as he rides above—
The madman whose delirium was love!
Doctored Professor of the "Joyful Science"
And soldier of impossible defiance,
Mortality oppressed his boundless youth
The stoned and hunted heretic of truth.
Stoned, he rose laughing, hunted, hunted Death
And ran it down gasping for its own breath,
Which knowing not pursuit, but to pursue,
From such unwonted heat in panic flew
Till cornered breathless in its native sewer,
The Tcheka, where it turned on its pursuer:
For Death was but another of his stunts
In order to be everywhere at once:
And those who helped him to so wide a grave
Buried themselves, the century to save!
Danger, his bride, to lose him, died of sorrow:
And by the sons she bore him, since that morrow
Was never known again, though they inquire
Through seas of blood and hurricanes of fire!

With lions' sinews may his lyre be strung,
As mine with mere Orlando-hide is hung,
By whom these wonders fitly shall be sung
To make amends to Spain for all the lies
An age of creeping Tartuffes in disguise,
For centuries have still been forced to spin
To cover the lewd haunch of Ann Boleyn,
And with smug incense to deodorize
Their pimping to a murderous cuckold's sin—

Which gave us first our famous unemployed
And now would sell our sons to Marx and Freud,
Our history, made one black Face-saving Lie
The Spanish Inquisition to decry,
Which slew less Jews with its protecting hand
Than Cecil's Ogpu[1] made them rich and grand
By murdering Christians for their wealth and land—
Now breeds this gluttonous dupe that can be fed
With the "Most Powerful Weapons" of the Red
So as to give sword-swallowers the gripes
And twinge the Ostrich in his envious tripes—
Since lying now, as far as Spain's concerned,
Into a Second Nature has been turned,
Lie fertilizing huge dyspeptic lie
Until to-day the Legend fills the sky,
Till Spanish priests on their twelve pounds a year
As "rich" and "worldly" courtesans appear[2]
To our pink Mitred Glabs of Guts and Suet
So thick they scarce can force their peepers through it,
When but to see the Carmelite who goes
Barefooted in the fierce Castilian snows
Would give them nightmares in their gouty toes,
Who sponsor Onanism and Divorce
And let the birthrate flounder on its course,
Whose Pickwickoid stupidity accrues
From idleness, fat livings, empty pews,
Whose smarmy ruse in fear of coming slaughter
Is mixing Vodka with the holy water;
Yet these who rave against the New Dictators
For shooting off a hundred agitators
Unruffled saw the butchery of Eire
As if it were the death of a Canary,
Approve the Russian spate of gore and filth
With Spies and Wreckers licking up the spilth—
If Stalin speaks the truth; if he does not,

[1] Walsingham, the head of Elizabeth's Gestapo, in a letter quoted by Froude, admits that the English were far more bloodthirsty in their persecution of the Catholic Irish, than the Spanish were with the Dutch protestants.

[2] Scale of salaries, Cardinal of Toledo £1,600 per annum. Archbishop of Canterbury £15,000!!

How then the bloodiest Wrecker tops the lot!
And blame the valiant Franco and his train
They would not have its counterpart in Spain
And to such cancerous growth of running sores
Preferred the amputation of the wars:
The Godless state of Russia they've commended
"As nearest yet to what our Lord intended"—
These Pickwickoid buffoons will smell you roses
Where even dunghill rats would hold their noses,
And though divorce was their first end and source
Though Onanism's now their next resource,
And next, who knows, to keep the same proportion
These canting thugs will sanctify abortion?
With compromise who've always pandered yet
Each royal and public weakness to abet,
The common lusts obligingly who shove—
Impeach their King (and Pope) for honouring Love!
Yet where was that Defender of the Faith
Whom ever lust or murder brought to scathe
Or through adultery ever came to grief?
It was for chivalry they sacked their chief
The chivalry that wipes out every stain—
(And worth it England's manhood to regain!)
A King too generous, direct, and manly
For fallen England or the likes of Stanley.
But what imports, so they can keep their place,
The Christian Family, the crown, the Race?
Just now, when every race should clear its decks,
And through the sky the thunder roars for wrecks,
When all the traitors are in place and power[1]
Life to deny, and Virtue to deflower,
And soul-destroying energies annex
The softening belly, and defile the sex,
Where Rome and Babylon received the shot
From Freuds and Marxes who were on the spot.
When the great trumpet sings the gates asunder

[1] This was written before the time of Fuchs, Pontecorvo, Otto John,
Alger Hiss, but the most biassed reader will have to admit that it
indicated them (Marx, Freud, and Einstein who gave us the atom
bomb, belonged to the same destructive *emigraille*).

And Christian virtue rides to face the thunder,
And bankrupt Progress, prostituted Science,
Are half with the Destroyer in alliance;
Where only virtue hammered out of steel
Tempered in ice and on the solar wheel
Honed to an edge, and spotless as its ray—
Can hope to hold against the world's decay—
Many of these can only feebly grin
To feel the poisons rioting within,
Who smile to see true Churches overthrown
And made as void and ugly as their own
When they of Saints and Angels stripped their Abbey
To fill with whiskered imbeciles, and flabby,
Frock-coated wiseacres in Alabaster—
The harbingers of Progress and Disaster,
The idols of a belly-worshipped people
Who've hoisted Carnal Comfort to the Steeple
And while the surfeit chokes them to the necks
Of housing, comfort, heating, food, and sex,
The like of which on earth was never seen
And carries luxury to the latrine,
More pomp and ritual paying to that shrine
Than ever yet to altars more divine,
And whom to punish, their own prayers are granted
Always to get exactly what they've wanted!
Free love, Free verse, Free thinking, contradictions
Of terms, involve them in far worse restrictions,
Tie up their natures worse, and cramp their souls
Than if like bears they were chained up to poles,
Till one and all they blare from night to morn
"Better by far that never we'd been born":
But whose own curates loud as they complain
Live fatter than a Cardinal in Spain,
Whose humblest vergers sleep in cotton sheets
And suck the sow of comfort by the teats.
The hardest sacrifice of those who sneer
At our brave martyrs slashed from ear to ear,
Is to be short of money, fags, or beer;
They dread no sudden knife-thrust in the ribs
Nor to be set on fire like human squibs,

Since communism has no fear of these
Who oil its way for it, and preach to please.
The "comrade" scorns such mounds of walking bunk
As roundly as he feared the Spanish monk,
Who with his blood could rout and overwhelm
The roaring horde of Moscow from the realm
And seat once more his Master at the helm:
As when Napoleon tried such tricks before
It was the priest that led the files of war.
But even Judas would disown his kin
In these betrayers of their Saviour's skin
Who dare to vilify the Church in Spain
And justify her holocausts of slain,
Crowding to swell the Regicidal cry
When the great Cross is reared against the sky—
Where there were no ground-rents, fat livings, feasts,
But only whips and scaffolds for the priests,
Who, different as the Living from the Dead,
Could lead their flocks as these by theirs are led
Where yet their blood the wave of conquests yeasts
And iron instead of pork's the stuff of priests,
Who fed on leavings, slept on wood and stone,
To rise in glory to the sacred throne . . .
Such, bestial comfort! are they boasted boons
To turn a race of heroes to buffoons:
And how would the red massacres compare
If Moscow should decide to launch them there
In England, where the blood's so cold and cruel
And years of smug repression stoke the fuel,
Where black misanthropy so fiercely clogs,
And love is squandered on the cats and dogs,
Go ask the red and black skins in our tanyard
Whether the cruel inquisitorial Spaniard
Or creeping Saxon, Pickwickoid and Kind,
Is more a master suited to their mind,
And when the Inquisition vetoed slavery,
What kind humanitarian plied the knavery?
Under whose rule the Red Man has survived
And Polynesian multiplied and thrived?
And where the Red Man and the Maori are

Who lived beneath the Philanthropic star?
Whole continents dispeopled of their race
By those who'll cant in Mussolini's face
When from the "human Wolf," the cursed Amharic,
He freed slave-races ten times less Barbaric—
And ask yourself how England would compare
Were the red Wardance to be started there?
Creating Dust-bowls with bad agriculture,
By killing forests, droughts to feed the Vulture,
At the same time with mountains of bolony
They'd ban the waving fields of Macaroni—
While they annex the Boer, invade the Gaucho,
Although of that the latter made a cow-show!
But still the Spaniard's empire on this earth
Has been in height as ours in sweeping girth
And, perpendicular as ours is level,
Affords less room or foothold for the devil.
His mission is to save as ours to clutch
And there's no country that we owe so much,
Who conquering more great powers than we have small
Has twenty times averted Europe's fall
As now she stands between us and the hell
Which no godless democracy could quell.
Our liberal democracy unturfed
The creeping conquered Saxon where he serfed
For the proud Norman and Unconquered Scot
Now decadent, the sissy and the sot,
Who like all underdogs when they get free
To bully smaller nations made his spree—
While Spain has mostly battled with the strongest
And in their rout her history's the longest.
Napoleon's strength was hamstrung with her iron
Before the mastiffs fell upon that Lion:
And Lenin's with Napoleon's godless star
Predestinately foundered from afar,
Both Revolutions as one failure seen
Whose godless altar was the guillotine.
Against the Carthaginian and the Turk
Whether from West or farthest East they work
(As Russia now) the Spaniard's is the call

When towering heathen odds on Europe fall:
Always to save her in her own despite
While protestants for Jew or Turk will fight
Or sit as we do now upon the wall,
Transporting armies she defeats, to crawl
Back to the battle that would whelm us all.
While in our smug humanitarian robe
We understock a quarter of the globe,
Spain will be always there against all odds
To bear the brunt, and rescue to the gods
More of the world from chaos and destruction
Than we can kiss with philanthropic suction:
Send more black souls to God like joyful rockets
Than we can crush and grind into our pockets,
Exterminating tribes as she preserves them
And swindling them as freely as she serves them,
As Mexicans and Filipinos show
But the poor Maoris are too scarce to know;
And still, whatever hurricane be hurled,
Preserving Europe, to preserve the world
Even as now, in this stupendous fight,
To save us almost in our own despite,
She gives the first wound that will surely rot
Even into the Kremlin's central spot,
While hypnotized and waiting to be shot
Our people only tried to stave the slaughter
By mixing with a little friendly water
The Vodka, when it seemed to grow too hot—
Their Church a Trojan Dray-horse to the plot.
But Spain, seraphic on the Ages' Rock,
Defied the thunder and returned the shock
From that divine sky-sundering sierra
That stands unshakeable in seas of Terror,
Two thousand years ahead of, and above
The world, amidst the thunderclouds of Love.
It saw the Hun, the Vandal, and the Arian,
The Reformation to the Proletarian,
Through Capitalism, stretch its sickening line,
And watched the jerks and jitters of its spine
As it lay vomiting its spawn of sharks

207

To cough its soul in Einstein,[1] Freud and Marx,
With liberal, democrat, and blond Barbarian,
And now the pacifist humanitarian,
(The bloodiest beast by nature misbegotten)
With anglican and calvinist gone rotten,
Their churches empty and their creeds forgotten,
Science gone bankrupt, Progress on the lurch,
And Socialism hanged on its own perch—
And stands to-day impregnable, as when
It was defended by eleven men
Who took the world (as Quiepo took Red Seville
Who out of Andalusia flogged the Devil)
When Christians gloried on the bloot-lit sand
And the Arena was our native land:
And saw the Cæsars sink their storm-red suns
And passed the joyful wisdom to their sons
To count its age by each world-heaving passion
Whatever form of Wowserdom's in fashion.
It was but yesterday it smashed the Huns
And now the crack through startled Russia runs.
The Turks before, the Bolsheviks to-day
Have crashed in bloody foam and rolled away:
And Bolshevism is but one wreck more
Its thunderstriking mole has piled ashore.
A million more it reaches to collect
Which makes its bastion out of Babels wrecked,
With all that was most modern in its prime
Or is like to be for all succeeding time.
For still the latest fashion and the mode
To her great scrapheap take the shortest road
Whose skeletons the more they're dashed and wrecked
Form huger bastions, further to project
And fortify against the outer world
The very keep at which their rage was hurled:
And Bolshevism forms but one more mole
To wreck whatever new mad force may roll
Against that towering fortress of the soul!

[1] This monstrous Tartuffiser won a Peace-prize from his fellow explosive-inventor, Nobel. The Hypocrisy of modern life is reflected in such a farce. It should always be remembered that it was Einstein, "the pacifist", who wrote to Roosevelt offering the Atom Bomb.

Book III

To my heroic Ex-Enemies, Hamish Fraser, ex-Communist
Kommissar of one of the toughest Units in the Whole International Brigade, now a Christian, and to Hugh Oloff de
Wet who flew for the Reds as a fighter pilot, and realised
the truth before he finished.

Scourged by the Prince of Horsemen from above,
Pursued by whizzing flies but not for love,
With suds of dripping on their blood-red beef
All groaning for the watery relief,
These captured rooineks[1] that perfume the path,
Before their lives, will clamour for their bath—
For water eared them with those scarlet fins
And water logged their boiled unhealthy skins:
Exposed to air for longer than they wish
They fare far worse than crocodiles or fish.
For like their politics their damned hygiene
Results the wrong way round from what they mean
Whose boomerang intentions still come back
With the same sickening and resounding whack:
From Soap to Sanctions nothing they apply
But they collect it in the Nose or Eye—
And of all stinks the devil ever cursed
The godless Saxon's toejam is the worst![2]
In washing as in life they are the same,
The Opposite rewards their dearest aim,
For Comfort cruelly themselves they vex
And for Security would break their necks,
For cleanliness they skirl with fearful hum,
To war for peace, aggressively they come,
And martyrs in each cause are nothing loth
With dirt and blood to illustrate them both.
Frustration the main theme of all their cults,

[1] Rooineks: i.e. rednecks, Afrikaans for Englishmen.

[2] The reek of a British Barrack room or Troopship takes a lot of
getting used to after the scentless Spanish army. I ascribe this to over-
eating, overwashing, and the use of butter instead of olive oil.

They wash and war with similar results,
Which makes their poets wish they'd not been born
And hold their kill-joy parents up to scorn
Whose error was not to abort them whole,
In body, as they managed with the soul,
For perished rubber dashed their early hopes
As sponsored by their Church and Marie Stopes;
With those strange eyes which never look but "peer"
And still to find the world is out of gear,
Which they'd reform regardless of the curse
That everything they change is for the worse,
Whose phobia for the Actual runs so high
(As Lenin saw) they'll perish for a Lie,
And never stop to ask the reason why,
To fight for "Liberty" who grant it least
And for "Humanity" to make a beast,
Whose third-rate morals always sympathize
Where there's most scope for villainy or lies,
And always with some moral pretext pat
For living with the morals of a Rat—
Whatever they would mend they botch the more,
And aggravate as children scratch a sore:
As women flog their brats to stop them crying
To every thud a fiercer howl replying—
They treat their lives, their sodden skins they scrub,
And seek their Bath as topers do the pub.
Of human Feelings underneath the sun,
Exasperation seems their only One—
Still with the world's realities at war
They live in them, as stranded fish ashore,
Yet in whatever villainy their heart is
It's always as the grossly "injured parties"—
It is for Right and Liberty they pong
And our poor noses that are in the wrong!
Though of this plight the Charlie makes a mystery
His case is simpler than the Natural History
From which his prophets spring (his Huxleys, Joads,
And Haldanes) skilful in the ways of toads
And axolotls, as they're helpless boobs
Outside their world of microscopes and tubes

And even then interpret Nature's laws
By taking the results to be the Cause.
Though in their fine experiments exact,
They take the negative to be the fact
Which is why "progress" in their own despite,
Harks to the primitive prenatal night,
And while a higher culture is their goal,
They mechanize and bestialize the soul,
And here the Charlie's greatest dangers lie
Accepting Science which has proved a Lie
As far as application is concerned.
So all his nature-study should be burned
If into dogma it must still be turned—
And sure by its colossal failure here,
Its worst fanatics should be taught to fear:
For to the very beasts (from germs to horses)
By which he would direct his earthly courses
He owes the very opposite of thanks:
Since it was Rozinante kicked his tanks,
And of all beasts in which his lore is slickest,
It was the microbes sized him up the quickest,
On his hygienic hide they fastened thickest—
No sooner did they glimpse this learned dunce
But "took him for an Englishman" at once,
And though the truth of it neither can twig
They see him little as he sees them big:
While them he magnified through lenses dim
And made like giants in his fancy swim,
They see him as despicable and small,
And straight upon him tooth and nail they fall:
Since from the best end of the microscope
(While he learned fear) they learned their strength and scope.
If all his science could be thus reversed,
'Twould make him happy as it makes him cursed,
And both in health and battle it is so—
They fare the best who least redoubt the foe:
If I feared germs I'd snuffle with the flu—
Or communists, with communism too.
Day Lewis to the Communist "feels small"
But nothing's made me feel so steep and tall:

With me such things are easy to determine
Who never felt this reverence for vermin
And all I know is, communists or germs,
He fares the best who never comes to terms!
So what between the Microbe and the Man
The Wowser must result an Also Ran
Who's got the Goat alike through his own meanness
Of human grandeur as of bestial wee-ness,
Plagued by the latter with a rage insane
To hunt the former with the hate of Cain,
While humanizing microbes in his mind,
Bacteriologizing human kind,
In whom no finer feelings he'll admit
Than actuate a woodlouse or a nit:
Not only in his Science and his Art
Identified with germs to play their part
In onslaught on the human form and face
And the preserving virtues of the race,
But also making war upon the past
All of its nobler lineaments to blast
Lest any human excellence transpire
To lift our heads an inch above the mire
To emulate, or even to admire:
For human contours, it will not allow
The brave man's thorax or the wise man's brow:
Small motives to great actions must be traced
And nature systematically debased,
Whose human outlines we must only follow
By feeling for what's negative and hollow,
Flattering every weakness we can find,
Condoning every baseness of the mind,
With faults for handles, seeking for the grip
To overthrow the noble horsemanship
The soul requires to dominate and charm
The bronco flesh, so restive to alarm,
And pitching both into the filth and mire
To cheapen them for slavery and hire—
The racket of the Invert and the Jew
Which is through art and science to subdue,
Humiliate, and to a pulp reduce

The Human Spirit for industrial use
Whether by Capital or Communism
It's all the same, despite their seeming schism,
In that for human serfs they both require
Limpness, servility, and lack of fire.
And that's the task of modern art and verse
Whose high-paid priests are certified perverse
From those whose race or sex degrades them most
Before they raise them to their envied post:
So that obsessed by their humiliation
They'll socialize their weakness to the nation,
Each, of his botches the self-conscious snob,
To flatter and instil them in the mob,
Rewarded with high honours by the state
For Charlotading all that's fine or great,
All valour, grace, and virtue to decry
And boost the pusillanimous on high:
And cheapening us first in our own eyes
By spitting on all values that we prize,
Grow fat upon the treacherous employ,
Each as a belled cabestro, or decoy,
With a gold medal clanking at his neck
To lure his fellows to their sale and wreck,
When cheapened, hypnotized, unmanned and cowed,
The gelded slave his "freedom" is allowed—
A tyranny far worse than blamed on Hitler
Whose chief oppression is of the belittler,
The intellectual invert, and the Jew,
Whose tyranny's the harder of the two,
Since not by force, but a more sure refinement,
Rather akin to solitary confinement,
They isolate the man who won't surrender
Or join their mass-crusades "against all splendour"—
And strong is he, with triple armour brassed,
Who will not hedge or compromise at last.
For the New artist is an Agent priced
To play on Man what Judas played on Christ,
In like humanitarian livery slinking
And in his purse the silver pieces clinking:
To cheapen him they drain their loving cup to—

That's what your defrocked Scoutmasters are up to!
But Nature still a boundary will fix
To such abuse. In this case it's the Styx.
For from the mere direction, gradient, pace,
It is not hard the destiny to trace
Of so much downward thinking: gravitation
Is their sole motor power, and our salvation:
The force of the Earth Mother pardons none
Who've not the counter-drive towards the Sun,
And not one Ampere of that force is found
In modern thought, which faces to the ground;
Which makes it only possible for Langdon
To see the pegs inferior hats are hanged on,
Who lectures us on "half-wits," so to rate men
Who foolishly (he thinks) believe in Great Men,
And of his own wit only uses half,
The part which faces nearest to the Calf,
Which can divide but cannot multiply
Its own proportions in the mental eye,
Sinking and shrinking only on itself
Though very small, and on a lower shelf,
With far less room beneath it than above it,
Although, up there, it would find few to love it:
It can allow some fellow half-wits space
But to do so must shut out half the race
Which beggars all his efforts to explain
What's happened at his barricades in Spain,
Routed by forces which, when Reds must fly,
Their legs acknowledge if their lips deny—
Greatness and Magnanimity of soul
Which from the start has had them up the pole!
Sheer mastery, unmixed with more ingredients,
Which Reds admit themselves—by their obedience,
Whenever they've a scarcity of brandy
Or foreign reinforcements are not handy:
What else explains Quiepo's enterprise,
Disarming regiments with his flashing eyes,
An unarmed rebel in an alien station
Gaoling the chiefs for insubordination
To what—when on their side were arms and law—

To what but sheer authority and awe!
Sheer greatness, that's above all grades of rank,
For which he only had himself to thank,
Weighing alone against the town of Seville
With tons of cutler's iron, plus the devil,
To prove the menial is a menial yet
However high he hoists his serviette
And that the types who live blaspheming tallness
Are those who show it up most by their smallness.
But the poor Charlie dooms his frantic strife
By shirking this first principle of life
With many more he struggles to deny
However hard they strike him in the eye,
And severed from their vitalizing force
He flounders ever downward on his course.
Like the Neanderthal who forms the text
Of his religion, he must follow next,
As holy relics though he keeps the bones[1]
Of that old ragamuffin of the stones—
As we do those of martyrs or of saints
To raise our faith or courage when it faints:
With his bashed skull to cheer his fated garrison
By means of a most flattering comparison,
To find in an abortion nature shelves
A freak as damned and ugly as themselves,
Whose downfall they mistook for evolution
And dogmatize with bloody persecution:
For as that sad degenerate of the rocks
Who co-existed with the manly stocks
Of the Aurignac, higher than our own
If height is in the vaulty forehead shown,
So the mad Charlie co-exists with ours
Which whets the envy of his failing powers,
And communism is his last fierce kick
To bring us down in the same mud to stick.
Hence too his hatred for the living past

[1] The Author has always sworn the Piltdown Skull on which all modern British Philosophy, Policy, Thought and Behaviour is founded was a disgraceful fake. (See *Revista Zoologica*, November 1933.) Even the most superstitious English scientists have been forced to admit this now.

That makes him feel so abject and aghast,
And though he trusts to his new fins and wings
For his salvation, which convenient things
Fish are too sensible, too wise the pigeons
To fabricate, like him, into religions—
He'll have to live protected like the Beavers,
And for a lake I recommend Geneva's
A sad anachronism without means
To live, supplanted by his own machines
Which though as dogs our bidding they obey,
Treat him (their worshipper) a different way—
For these machines, and daily they come faster,
Are plainly looking for a better master:
They drink his sweat, and chuck him out of work,
And drive him to the pistol and the dirk:
As one who treads on his own garden rake
It strikes him on the forehead like a snake,
So we behold his cannon and his tanks
Turn on him with a nancy offspring's thanks
From which our hand a treble thunder spanks:
They jilt him in the battle and the need
And in our hands rebound with vengeful speed,
As if they'd got his freudian lore by heart
Perversely primed to their unfilial part,
To turn and rend their bent and broken sire
And spread his mouldy fossils in the mire
For future mutts to treasure and admire:
His impetus is not to breach the tomb
But drag his rival down to share his doom,
For which he uses all his logic, science
Every new gadget, every new appliance,
In knowledge, economics, and hygiene,
Always to shuffle lower than he's been—
Drugging himself with that hypnotic shout
Of "progress" (which he knows is fear and doubt)
Down, down, down, down—until he's down and out!
When Nelson held his glass to his blind eye,
Unpommified, it was to do or die!
But his descendant does it as a rite
Whenever something Obvious heaves in sight:

To shun the Actual nobody more smart,
To dodge the Obvious is his native art,
For both insult him with derisive grin
From his environment and from within:
Whose gluttony all mixtures can sustain
Save what is actual, evident or plain—
"The Atlas eater with a jaw for News"
Whose ostrich mind no mischief can refuse,
Whose scarlet ears and mediumistic mind
Express for Propaganda were designed,
In Spain or Russia swallowing every farce
In which he plays the leading Role of Ass,
Who still where he has "peered" with his pink eyes
A proverb for credulity supplies,
For proverbs he has made the Ass look poor
To symbolize the booby and the boor,
Where peering eyes and ears of monstrous size
"To take one for a Britisher" implies:
Since all his Pelman course and monkey's glands
With which the Charlie intellect expands,
His lore of vitamins, the germs and mites
To which he pays his more fantastic rites—
From all this Voodoo there results a sap,
You will not find his equal on the map:
For all things shining generous or clear
He has low motives and a knowing leer,
And were a phoenix from its fragrant pyre
To blossom he would piddle on the fire,
Whom all things bore except to gloat or gape
At tales of murder, cruelty and rape,
Whose only living folk-lore, for his grovels,
Is canine limericks and detective novels
Where (as in Spain) he sleuths the obvious guilt
From the Red villain, proving to the hilt
Some unsuspecting Christian is the crook
And always the least abject in the book:[1]
Until the squint into his nature grows
Scenting the drainpipe to the open rose—

[1] An extraordinary fact in a doomed race is that it always prefers a
lie to the truth. Lenin understood this: it formed the main part of his
"Technique".

And now the Hero of this War on Truth,
The "National Type" becomes the sneaking sleuth:
Who lofty monuments can never spy
Save with a dog-like itch to lift his thigh,
Traitor to life and that which moves the spheres
Whose music never sounded in his ears,
For Mischief is the only joy he seeks
Or brings the colour to his flabby cheeks:
To make life easy is his one resource
With sodomy, abortion, and divorce—
As some poltroon to tame a noble horse
Instead of vaulting to the risky heights
Runs off complaining that it kicks and bites,
Starves it into a hat-rack, kills its pride,
And strings its hams before he dares to ride:
And then observing it is spoilt and lame
Would have all other riders do the same
For envy draws the supercilious sneer
With which he views their galloping career
For none he deems deserve the joyous strife
Which he gave up for his ignoble life:
Pursuing honour even to the grave
Where he debunks the valiant and the brave
With abject lies their graves to picnic-litter
And tapeworm in the charnel for a titter.
Were this not so, what else could move his brain
To sabotage the Victory of Spain
Which like a miracle from nothing born
To Nightmare-ridden Europe shows the Morn.
To arm the villain with his gold he flies
And every day to circulate his lies,
In all the leading Journals of the times
To blame us for the Reds' Subhuman crimes,   •
Guernica dynamited from within
He lays to Franco's aeroplanes the sin,
And with humanitarian fuss makes bold
To "save Bilbao's children" (and its gold!)[1]
That with the looted treasuries of Spain
Good Marxists may not want the best Champagne

[1] Prieto sailed from there in the yacht *Vita* with some £60,000,000

In the Parisian Cafes where they reign:
Then, twenty thousand troops dismayed with fear
Transporting round to hack us in the rear!
To serve these ends he runs his murderous guns
And robs the Spanish mothers of their sons.
Guernica! even were the lie not patent
Still his hypocrisy would be as blatant
Who said no word (the sanctimonious Caviller!)
When Huesca, Cordoba, Granada, Avila
Valladolid, Pamplona, twenty more
Far from the zone or interest of war,
Were bombed and shattered many months before,
Had these been strongholds of the sons of Marx
And turned to shambles by those ugly sharks
So that to bomb them into smithereens
Would almost be improvement to their scenes—
What Caterwaulings would have filled the Deans!
Had Spain's unarmed and slaughtered Christian Dead
Been Abyssinian slave-drivers instead,
Had they been thugs or Papuan head-hunters
What Indignation would have filled the grunters
For the sly Pickwick has a sliding lid
"Tut, tut," he cries, "the Obvious is hid
But even if it be as we observe it
The victims must be wicked to deserve it:
To Landru's victims and to Bluebeard's wives
Must be ascribed the monsters' wicked lives
And if we take this broader view in Spain
The victims have least reason to complain."
His noble fleet, once noblest in the trade,
To gunmen and to gangsters lent its aid,

belonging to the Spanish people. On the demand of the "Campesino",
Lister of the Lister Brigade was had up in Moscow for raping five of
these children when he was drunk. He was able to prove that they were
all Catholics, that is to say "fascists," and got off scot-free, the Pasionaria
abetting him. If you look up English papers of that time, you will find
these kidnapped children, some of whom were taken to England, were
misrepresented as Republicans. These facts, and some amusing ones
about the Pasionaria, are to be found in *Listen Comrades* by General
Emilio Gomez, "el Campesino", by far the best of the Spanish Red
Generals, who recently escaped from Russia.

To refuge thieves and loot across the main,
Which he denied to the best blood of Spain,
As I have seen, on Red Valencia's shore,
The mother and the child in vain implore—
To be sent back into the murderous flood,
And there to wallow side by side in blood,
And that's the pretty sight that fills my eye
When "Save the little Children" is his cry!
All of his reasoning adroitly maimed
Wherever villainy must be acclaimed,
And even in his own home he must glory
As the damned sleuth of a detective story,
For the mad poisoner he does not look
But blames it all upon the poor old cook—
The poor Arms-manufacturer gets blamed
For what old Angell preaches unashamed:
For such as he no sort of blame will get
Though to the mine they've laid, the hugest yet,
They manage the Genevan fuse to set.
But peace will follow in the soldiers' spoor
As pacifism wades in human gore.
Directness always conquers indirectness
And cocksureness will smash the mere hen-peckness
Of such as Eden: were he not a "sleuth,"
Who'd be our laughing stock to eld and youth—
Were he our heavyweight, say, like Joe Beckett
The horizontal timepiece of the Count:
But as a sleuth, the cosmos, he may wreck it,
And still his popularity will mount!

So John Bull breathes in subterrene intrigue
And hangs around the coffin of the League,
That sheeny club of communists and masons
Where Pommies' ears serve for spittoons and basins
In which to wash the grime from bloody paws
Fresh from the massacres of human laws,
While from all living zest he always warps
To bind his faith to every rotten corpse—
The League, the Soviet, his macabre dance
With the corrupted Mafia-gangs of France,

That shakes herself to bits at every jig—
False teeth, glass eyes, and pestilential wig!
For which wild orgies of necrophilism
He'll have to pay with worse than rheumatism:
Not Rowland Ward, the Prince of Taxidermy,
Could ginger up the moth-eaten and wormy
Trophies that he insists on bringing home
Whenever on the peacepath he would roam:
For the last twenty years—ever since Chanak
He seems to've got the weevil in his bannock:
Ireland, Manchukuo, Egypt, Palestine,
Against the Actual still he takes his line;
Now thanking recent friends for rendered aid
He bombs the Arabs, whom his Jews invade,
Yet turns on Mussolini bitter censures
Because against old enemies he ventures.
In Abyssinia—all its words reversed
About the Emperor, whom late it cursed
As tyrant, slaver-king, and bandolero,
Our Press then bills him as a martyr-hero:
But with dud promises that came to zero,
Had they not egged along this sable chieftain
To raise the parasol and drum the beef-tin,
He would have kept his kraal with guys that play fair,
Who now is half forgot-about in Mayfair
No more the "rage," but moved from door to door
Politely round the Foreign Office floor
Where he goes begging—what they rooked him for!
As if such lessons in humiliation
Were not enough to cause some hesitation,
Straightway in Spain, as if intent on Hell,
Against a Nation, he upholds a Smell!
There's not a failure reeking to the sky
He has not had his nose in since Versailles,
Through still increasing failures swept along,
The merrier he, the fiercer that they pong:
Not Sawny Bean nor Landru filled their Cupboard
With such strange catsmeat as this Brother Hubbard
Has scavenged upon his funereal quest
Until the very graveyards groan for rest.

Ever since Chanak on the downward grade
Britannia's trident now a graveyard spade.
For in the modern world, not arms nor wealth,
(As Spain has shown) but nationhood, is health
And that which wins the crisis or the quarrel,
So far from economical, is moral.
Gold in the present world stampeding flies,
And Sanctions are for Left-ward-squinting eyes
Where only chaos and destruction lies.
In actualities not worth a louse—
Such politics are for the Boarding House
Where Marx and Lenin their existence spent
In quarrelling with landladies for rent,
For half of their experience was learned
In swindling charwomen of what they earned,
And they with pans and broomsticks learned that strife
They later put across in modern life
With that same hatred of the middle class,
(Through owing rent) that they have brought to pass
Through all the world where lodgings must be paid
Or any sort of decency obeyed.
In Russia any mountebank got round,
As everywhere where liberals are found,
And where Rasputin spilled his old Voodoo
No wonder Marx and Lenin worked their New;
From two old Sheenies harassed for their board
And forced to break their stocking-treasured hoard,
From time to time, against their grudging will—
That grudge arose the mighty world to fill,
So easily in Godless man infected
By any rancour, and the worse subjected
The meaner and more abject is its source:
From this the Marxian theory draws its force,
With patience canvassing each doss-house lodging
Where there's a grudge to pay, or rent for dodging,
And though about as modern as Stonehenge,
And ancient as the feeling of revenge,
It owes the huge momentum of its spate
To that it can collect the petty hate,
Boredom, greed, envy of the World in one,

And vomit it blaspheming to the sun
With such results as Barcelona shows,
And ruined France, Karfunkelled[1] through the nose,
With Russia as the Model that presages
Their New Jerusalem, the Wreck of Ages,
Like some wrecked parlour in a third-rate pension,
Though raised to an Olympian dimension,
With the stale smell of cabbage soup, spilt gravy,
And dirty linen to depress the slavey
All chucked in drab disorder through the house
As by some foreign lodger with a grouse.
Marx's whole knowledge of the earth and sun
Was of a boarding house for exiles run
With dodging rent as the chief role of man
And being as much a nuisance as one can:
Which is why Hitler gives them leave to quit:[2]
Rather than be with his own broomsticks hit
By his own lodgers, firing all such boarders
Before, instead of after, the disorders.

[1] "Blum" was an alias for Karfunkelstein.

[2] Compared with our beloved Russian allies, who never let dissidents
escape or emigrate, even Hitler was, at this time, comparatively human,
since he did not impede but encouraged the exodus of the *emigraille*
which has cost England her empire and atom-bomb secrets.

Book IV

The Patagonians of humans first
Discovered Communism, and were cursed
Through all the centuries to stay the same
Which Christians filled with energy and flame
And still continue other cults to shade
As in this last ineffable crusade;
The termites, too, who tunnel in the sod
Set up a like Equality for God,
Expel their males to soar in shining rings
Because they are creative and have wings
And feel the love of high and fiery things—
And run a red republic on the lines
Attempted at the Rio Tinto Mines,[1]
For of all creatures by the stars accursed
The miner and the burrower come first,
Though of all navvies, egg or woman born,
They take the highest wage in cash or corn:
Whether it be their toil that warps their worth
Or their own Nature drives them under earth,
There, while the Devil Stakhanovs their crew,
Labour for labour's sake is all they do,
So their drab soviet underneath our drains
Stagnant to all eternity remains
Where changeless for eleven million years,
They've quarried with no music in their ears,
Iconoclasts with Marx-obedient jaws,
Destroying all that is above their laws,
Who gnaw down churches lest the Christians pray,
Who eat the finest canvasses away,
Reducing libraries to the same cud
To build their dingy barracks in the mud:
Life cannot change them if it would,
Who to the Useful sacrificed the Good,
Who to the belly sacrificed the eye

[1] Since serving as a volunteer and a private attached to both the
S.W.B. and the R.W.F. with many Welsh miners for my comrades,
and since I had the honour of fighting the valiant Asturian miners, I
make two very great exceptions to my generalization about miners.

And to the common what is rare and high.
For he who puts mere Labour to the fore
Will drive the finer angels from the door
And slay the myth by whose creating fire
Adam was first ignited from the mire—
The finest workers and the first on duty,
Who subject labour still to love or beauty,
Win far more grace and far less duties shirk
Than those who make a gospel of their work:
And man's true need, beyond another thing
In ruling nature, is to shine and sing,
Wherever this is so, his triumph's plain
As you may see in liberated Spain.
No drudgery performed this peerless feat
The surplus of a million tons of wheat,
But normal effort between song and prayer
Though only half the harvesters were there—
Less than on strength or numbers, work depends
On mood: and that, upon the purposed ends:
Less than on effort, work depends on style
Which leaves that groaning Sisyphus a mile,
And fresh at eve its finished task can slacken off,
While through the night each grim, shock-working Stakhanov,
His mess of cabbage freezing on the hob
Must wrestle with his uncompleted job:
Till when his tractor's finished, it back-fires
Three times, and with a dismal cough expires:
In vain his spanner turns, his hammer thuds,
For of five tractors, four of them are duds,
And those that manage to the fields to climb
Rattle to pieces in a fortnight's time,
Creative rhythm shuns their blistered hands
And is a thing no Fiscal understands
While style and unity and emulation
Inform each clean rejuvenated Nation,
Wherever there's a Leader to rebel
Against the outworn socialistic Hell,
And muzzle up the soul-destroying Lie
Which Lenin was the first to Magnify
As "our most mighty weapon" to disarm

And hypnotize the nations to their harm,
Of doped electorates to turn the votes
To suicidal razors at their throats,
And with that prehistoric dinosaur
The voting public, which can judge no more,
When they have tanned its hide and stuffed its corse,
To work the blarney of the Trojan horse:
As now in England the Triumphant Lie
Is mesmerizing multitudes to die
By radio, by newspaper, and, worse,
In literature, in painting, and in verse,
Where modern Southeys, to the mode who clown,
For going Red, can bum the Laureate crown:
While unbought men, who think and understand
And indicate the actual with their hand,
Like criminals are shunned throughout the land—
As for myself I glory in my crime—
Of English poets first in all my time
To sock the bleary monster in my rhyme,
As first in arms to face this Prince of Wowsers
And drive the bullets through his baggy trousers,
And now to bring, with his bug-eaten head,
The tidings that Democracy is dead.

Now see amongst the democratic races
How "spies" and "wreckers" fill the highest places
And how this system, decades under way,
Increases still in bloodshed every day,
And how much love or loyalty is bred
Between the bolshy leader and the led
Where all is suspect, what you take or give,
And only abject boot-lickers can live
Where he who spies upon his dearest friend
The butchers of the Soviet commend,
To keep the stream of victims swelling tidal
And sate the bloodlust of their bloated idol,
To whose record of murder, graft, and shame
The fetishes of cannibals are tame.
Utility, in its own place and hour,
Of human virtues is a humbler flower

But when deluded by the Wowser's lies,
To force and brutal insolence it flies—
Utility no more, but its reverse,
Can be the world's most sanguinary curse.
So Bolshevism, if it comes to all,
As universal punishment will fall.
The Writing has been long upon the Wall.

Sancho, the servant, was a great success
But when he ruled the island made a mess,
Nor can you raise the menial to a crown
Though on his pate you pulled Olympus down!
Work's but the simplest way of getting bread
No hardship but a privilege instead:
No special dignity to it attaches—
Though more than to the plight of selling matches,
To living on a woman, pimping, thieving,
Or printing lies for other folk's believing.
That one can crank a car or wash a dish up
Entitles nobody to roast a bishop,
With rights of life and death over one's neighbour
To rape, to burn, to torture, and belabour.
It may be true of the Slavonic nation,
But two, in Spain, can play at "liquidation."
The Left possessed the all-compelling arms
Which drove us from the factories and farms
Strike after strike was ordered and compelled
And it was death if honesty rebelled.
For they resented willingness and skill
And that we could go fighting up the hill—
As if a race of drones with guns and knives,
Crazed with a creed that grudges and deprives,
Can better men in whom the Faith survives
Or clean the world before they clean their lives.
The reformation of the whole world's sin
Is not in other people, but within.
They'll tell you that the workers of the land
Are not on Franco's side with heart and hand,
And on "coercion" blame our eager toil
To raise the ruined wall or till the soil.

But of all bans the worst coercion still
Is that which keeps the worker from his skill,
All must that forced ineptitude refuse
Which grudges prowess even to the thews,
But in its hot intolerance more blind,
Forbids the triumphs of the heart and mind.
Nought raised the wrath of these blood-sucking skunks
More than the adoration of the monks
To whom (as envious of a lovely wife)
They grudged the Resurrection and the Life
And first by slander: then, when it was safe,
By murder, strove the living Church to waif:
For joyous gifts (however proud or rare)
Which drudgery or thieving cannot share,
The Fortunate their malice had to bear—
And foremost of these luxuries was prayer:
But sculpture too and painting felt their ire
And only what was priced escaped the fire!
But when the Right Hand got them by the scruffs
How pious grew these base bug-eaten toughs—
With church bells ringing to deceive our Deans
With psalmody of Prietos and Negrins,
White-stoled militia-men in mystic swoon
And Largos chanting Aves to the moon!
And as they travesty Religion, too,
They make a ghastly parody of you,
Sweet privilege, now, in every field or street
The easiest to come by and to meet,
Labour, the little sister of the poor,
The saint who scares the prowler from my door—
Say, was it you that shut the baker's store
And set the dram shop in this red furore
With blood-shot eyes and methylated breath
Dispensing fierce delirium and death?
Did "Labour" strew this garbage in the street
That must lie stinking there, until defeat
Lets in our cleansing strength, the reek to whelm,
Like Hercules to this Augean realm?
These breadless queues of women in the rain
Who through the night of famine wait in vain

228

To be dispersed with buffetings and kicks,
Till hopelessly they gravitate again
Like silent spectres waiting by the Styx
Without their freighting penny, while Despair,
A harsher Charon, heedless of their prayer,
Raises a rifle-butt, his threatening oar,
And drives them backwards from the hungry shore
With filthy curses and insulting jokes;
While from his single fang a stump there smokes
Of horse-dung wrapped in newspaper unclean,
Before their eyes with tantalizing mien
He gnaws his crust and wolfs his stale sardine
Already bathed in phosphorescent sheen,
And tilts the bottle to his lips obscene
That have the fiery stench of gasolene,
While, music for his meal, with muffled groans
A mile along the filthy pavement drones
A syncopated orchestra of crones—
Yes, crones, at fifteen years: and even after
As dead to sorrow as immune to laughter!
These sights are propagated in your name
And human beings sold to worse than shame—
Far other was to be the wondrous hour
That saw "the people" absolute in power,
But when there was no more to slay or rob
Of whom or what was alien to the mob,
Not all the loot of museums or banks
Could prop that drunken monster on its shanks:
When all the blood of half-a-million slain,
Unarmed and innocent, had proved in vain
A spark of living vigour to infuse
In its slack sinews, and anæmic thews;
And when once absolute in power and pelf
With nothing there at all except itself,
All opposition crushed into the mud,
Still fiercely goaded by the thirst for blood
The flabby hydra, rabid with self-hate,
Now falls upon itself its lust to sate—
No Nero ever scourged the brute so black
With weals of crimson tigering its back

As this self-worshipping disastrous god
Itself has punished with its own red rod,
And now abjectly conscious of its loss
Implores the saving mercy of the Cross.
For man without a God, himself will crown
And so much lower than himself cringe down—
For still our moral height will rise or fall
By what we worship, so we stand or crawl—
As those in Barcelona thought it fine
To feed live victims to man-eating swine,
As those who rifled graves, dead nuns to raise,
Defiling nature in yet viler ways:
But whose own image when they contemplate
They fall into a frenzy of self-hate
Abjectly scared—and always far too late!
It was not "liberty" that thus could level
Mankind in common bondage to the Devil
Nor yours, kind Labour, was this ghastly birth
Of squalor—though to camouflage the stain,
Our intellectuals take your name in vain;
Only where Franco rules you seem to shine
Whose influence reaches to our foremost line;
For you'd be murdered on the other side
(Efficiency insults their tender pride):
And any fool who pauses to examine
The artificial dirt and man-made famine
They spread around, this simple truth can learn
From villages they've had no time to burn
Before retiring: till their hoarded dirt
From your white apron and your azure skirt
Suddenly seems to vanish from the region—
Like "Internationals" before the Legion:
And where oppressive to the nose and lung
That everlasting smell of human dung
That haunts their cities, like a fog has hung,[1]
Which seems to follow everywhere they roam

[1] The extraordinary result of complete licence was that people openly
excreted and urinated on the spot, in the streets and on the pavements,
like dogs in London. In Toledo, after the relief, a fine of 50 pesetas had
to be imposed before the rabble became "street-trained" once more.

As if to make their spirits feel at home—
Now on the morning air like amber roves
The long-forgotten scent of baking loaves.
As when the Bride her new home has possessed
Where the poor Bachelor has done his best—
Within two hours the sloven Cook must pack
And the sleek, thieving flunkey gets the sack:
With the accumulated dust of years
The cobweb in the corner disappears:
The new-scoured china shimmers on the rack
And the clean table flaunts a glossy back,
Which faithful quadruped had suffering lain
Ringwormed with saucer-marks as if in pain,
But now may prance, the race-horse of the room:
While the proud carpet, snorting to the broom,
Takes its first sunbath since it was laid down—
And as it's with a house, so with a town,
Where your deft fingers discipline restore
At half the price that Muddle cost before!
In the munition works, the 'phone-exchange,
Surprised machines, ecstatic to the change,
Begin to hum with ardour new and strange:
But finer still, at harvest on the flat,
To see you reaping in your wide straw-hat,
Broad-smiling as I pass, as if you know me,
The brown Mireille! after the Red Salome!

Book V
(*To Edith Sitwell, D.B.E.*)

Calm in the solitude while armies die
The Guadarramas sweep the western sky
Where tragic suns in Crucifixion slow
Bleed rubies on the silver saws below,
Or with a flash of bayonets, all as one,
The peaks salute the resurrected sun,
Around whose miracles of death and birth
Seraphic colours glorify the earth,
While through the green of an ethereal lake
To which the palest emeralds seem opaque,
The trawling vapours, crimson, orange, gold
Like cherubim their solar King enfold,
While violet glooms in gorgeous ruin soar
To surf in amber up the rosy shore:
Where now like almond blossom, now like hair
The pink and gold effeminize the air,
Yellow to green, and green to purple turning,
With one red circle in the centre burning
Which dies to give the glittering armies light
And valour for their battle through the Night:
And is reborn their myriads to unite
In the tremendous sapphire of the Day
Into whose width they've burned the Night away;
Those raindrop soldiers of his golden storm,
Each a small sun, repeat his mystic form,
And as they drew their being from his death,
So with their dying animate his breath,
Drawn into one by their immortal Sire,
To swell his rising hurricane of fire.
The Soldiers, too, like stars or drops of rain,
Who drew their burning life from martyred Spain
When in her Master's wounds she died again
To kindle them like stars upon the plain,
Now die into her resurrected Sun
Out of a myriad deaths reviving One
Whose wounds they wear, whose image they repeat,

The bludgeoned head, the torn and ragged feet—
And there, the final victory attained,
Behold the world by suffering explained
To perfect understanding, the supreme
Simplicity, of which those only dream
Who, shunning pain, would baulk the fiery beam:
But which (an angel with sustaining wings)
Acceptance of the Utmost surely brings,
And of our destiny can crown us Kings.
So while the enemy from bad to worse
Reduce the social wrongs they would reverse
And while they battle for "improved conditions"
In the blind faith of chemists and statisticians,
Denying us upon the pain of death
The burning realism of our faith,
We rather battle for improved positions
(Here, as on high) or captives and munitions—
With our brave creed two thousand years ahead
Of their slow Progress, which they've thrashed half-dead,
And have to push behind, if not to carry—
But which, as we advance, we leave to tarry,
The slowest mule, if willing, of our train
Who, left alone, will catch us up again . . .
For life and history are heroic things
And formulas can only clip their wings.
To no set theory will they move aright
However well it reads in black or white:
But with the sagas and the myths they'll run
Rejoicing with the seasons and the sun,
Whose theme and end and origin are One,
In sacrifice, in rite, in holy pageant
From earliest man predicted and imagined,
All variations of the single theme,
And consummated in the Act supreme
Which gave a name, a Person, and a soul
To the concerted purpose of the Whole,
When from the tree was sawn the "Golden Bough,"
As, whispering, all its withered leaves avow,
To shape the Cross that towers above us now!
From the white peaks across the mesa brown,

Where the low sun ignites on tower and town,
Where, faint and white, the long horizons reel
To reach the dwindled limits of Castile,
Coasting the amphitheatre of snow,
This eagle sees, along the far plateau,
Where crawls the battle in a fleecy shroud,
All in slow motion, like a morning cloud
Caught sleeping on the mesa: in the will
Of its internal cyclones clutched and still,
Hang colonnades of dust: or slow dissolving
Into the stainless azure, rise revolving;
Where detonates the life-destroying doom,
The sunshine silvers on a fading plume:
And the horizon seems, so far away,
A frieze of sunny clouds or frozen spray,
To be the work of seraphim at play:
While in its smoke with sobs of choking breath
Two giant forces copulate with death.
And as they fight, in one back-spraining ring
Hooping their spines like scorpions curved to sting,
Their creaking vertebrae, like rattled chains,
Hooked by their limbs as by earth-heaving cranes,
One in the violence of all earthly lusts,
To blind instinctive appetite who trusts,
To feed his guts, to satiate his sex
And wreak his hatreds, would the skies annex
And careless whether as his tomb or crown
Upon his head would drag creation down:
The other, vowed the heavens to uphold
And guard the gates of intellectual gold,
The labour of his fathers fair to see
And of his sons the heritage to be,
Still fights to keep the human concept whole,
The myth its aura, and the truth its soul!
But in their strife, unconscious as they rage on,
Each from the other catches his contagion—
The one by heroism oft inspired,
His foe as oft by desperation fired;
As if his soul into the flesh could strike,
Each in the other conjures up his like;

With rags of flesh upon their nails and teeth
They wrestle now above and now beneath,
And both so foul with blood and soot and dust,
And one by hate, the other by disgust
So unified, by smoke so densely screened,
You scarce can tell the angel from the fiend.

How thrilling sweet, as in the dawn of Time,
Under our horses smokes the pounded thyme
As we go forward; streaming into battle
Down on the road the crowded lorries rattle
Wherein the gay blue-shirted boys are singing,
As to a football match the rowdies bringing—
But of this match the wide earth is the ball
And by its end shall Europe stand or fall:
Cresting the rise, through dimly vapoured screens,
We hear the crackle of the death-machines,
But dwarfed by height and distance, it might be
A summer veld-fire that we hear and see,
Which drought, or some Red labourer set alight
To spoil the pasture or revenge a slight.
Through rolling smokewreaths, there, like ant-hills, rise
The koppies in the nitre-breathing skies,
While, in the troops, we see such turmoil reign
As in the tiny creatures of the plain.
Now like singed beetles lurch the coming Tanks
Followed by seeming ants, amid whose ranks
Fall cinders as they simmer here and there
Blown sidelong by the whiffs of torrid air,
As heat had brought them humming from their hives
To save their hoarded harvests with their lives—
But steel the harvest, bullets are the grain
They gather there in gaping jaws of pain.
While in the air with equal skill and ease,
Performing on their terrible trapeze,
The cruising gun-birds trim the sunny breeze,
Like swifts, and rollers, and meropidae,
Whom burning grass has lured from far away,
When through the smoke each fork-tailed beauty flies
To hawk the roasted insects as they rise.

Past dead men lying nonchalantly round
As if in brief siestas on the ground,
The horses, trotting, lift the town in view,
And thunder loudens, hammering the shoe
Of the Red Horse, so soon perhaps to pass,
The world for pampa, with its men for grass,
Whose shrieking whinny now our spirits hear
As down the widened valley we career
To sweep the falling city in the rear.
Past wounded men returning back, whose cheer
Rings like a ghostly whisper in the ear,
While to the left the rocky tempest raves
In which the cannon plough their jagged caves
And masonry is rumbled like the waves,
As if the world with undulating spine
Would imitate the heavings of the brine,
While architecture flies in smithereens,
The houses cataract into ravines,
And the steep rampart, with a roll of thunder,
As a great dam had burst itself asunder,
With men and rocks, a terrible moraine,
Goes avalanching downwards to the plain.
But nearer yet, and we are in the storm
Before their battered rearguard can reform—
While running bolshies fall upon their face,
Some stop to fire, reloading as they race,
Suddenly doubling as you make their pace,
So where you thought to slash the bulging nape
It is a face you widen in its gape,
To whose fierce shock your jolted elbow rings
And like a tuning-fork, your sabre sings,
The numbing blow, in its collected force,
Trebled by the momentum of the horse.

But scarce the Moors could our advantage prize,
When suddenly, as one to breast the rise,
A score of tanks were on them by surprise,
Pillioned with infantry that crept or clung
To their broad haunches, as to crabs their young;
Straight in our flank, where vigilance was tame,

They grumbled down the cornfield, spitting flame.
Many fell dead, while others in a sham
Lay waiting there to board that mortal tram,
Till nine or ten, from all sides running in,
The shelter of the cupola could win:
Half to the human team devote their blades
Or shock them from their vantage with grenades:
While others hugging to its shell so fast
They keep in shelter of its withering blast,
Work on the plunging monster: till at last
A pick is struck into the running belt,
Which has it soon revolving on the veld
Like a spent top: blankets and petrol, then,
And a great fire exploding, while our men
Rush backward: and the brainyell of the crew
Locked in and trapped, comes yodelling wildly through.
So are two others served: while of the score
The rest, retiring, leave one cripple more
Against the skyline, where in loose array
They move like angry pachyderms away.
Now with four Russian prisoners they pass—
The strange experiments in human glass
Blown out of shape by oratory gas:
Talking with whom we fail a self to find—
Men without God, the eunuchs of the mind,
Grown embryos, that life has left behind:
Far from the old "Red Square," who lose their way
By night, their combativity by day—
If ever they have aught for which to fight
Except their inequality in right.[1]
Reared for the news-reel and film-propaganda—
Were these the guys to face the fierce Aranda?
When in their myriad parachutes they sail
Like thistle-down upon the social gale
So wonderful to see upon the screen—
Contingencies are banished from the scene:
But should they launch such lunar tactics here
A pheasant-drive the battle would appear;

[1] The disproportion of pay in the Russian "egalitarian" Army between
officers and men, compared with other countries, is almost astronomical.

With camera-men for generals, for their foe
Hair-bristling audiences in panting row,
They were not reared for battle, but for show:
While from some grating underneath their feet
The photo-grinder "shoots" them in the street,
They tower sky-high as over us they go
Stamping hobnailed upon our heads below;
Launched from the screen straight out into the "gods"
Their armoured tanks go over us like clods,
To whose repeated unresisted shock
Our bourgeois gooseflesh creeps, our senses rock:
To the same tactics on the field they trust
Conceiving opposition to be dust,
But at the first resistance are non-plussed.

Now the Red airmen profit by the lapse
Of ours, their fearful cargoes to collapse.
This "open town", lately by them defended
Now to its very base they start to rend it:
Niagaras of smoke, reversed in act,
Leap from the ground in roaring cataract,
While high above their fringes of bitumen
Their distant outlines that the rays illumine,
In languid innocence, parade the blue
As if unconscious of the work they do,
So Sunday beauties walking up and down
Sow fire and brimstone all around the town,
And leave, when from the Vega they depart,
The senses whirling and the jagged heart.
And watching them, so lately flushed with power,
We feel our helplessness above us tower
High as a great sierra through the air,
Which only can be shifted by a prayer—
For see, our squadron crests the climbing rack
And hurtles to the hurricane attack.
Now, at the first to shoot its earthward gyre
A windmill churning to a gale of fire,
The rest makes off pursued by vengeful wings,
With pawn-like chasers covering their Kings.
As when the owls rise from the burning wheat,

Dazed by the light, and flustered by the heat,
The fork-tailed rollers flash with sky-blue quills
And rag the heavy moper with their bills;
In cruel fun they loop around their butt,
Till in some hole his ruffled wings can shut—
So by the chasers harried through the sky,
Headed for home, the heavy bombers fly,
And more than one, before his nest is found,
His upward-rushing shadow will confound,
And spread, in blazing fragments, on the ground.
On roofs and steeples flying and alighting
Like a spread fire, the flag of Spain igniting
Gains on the other fires the foe had lit
As ever when a town they're forced to quit;
For fire's the Reds' habitual farewell
Where they have time to leave a blasted hell—
Irun, Guernica, Cangas, Teruel,
And ninety more, the ghastly tale can tell:
How not content with murder, rape, and pillage,
They would raze out the name of every village
They have defiled, and burn away the traces
Of worse, with arson—so to save their faces:
Then if some British pressman should be handy—
From a safe distance, priming him with brandy,
To scoop their story in his red receivers,[1]
Pointing indignantly, the bloody rievers
Blame their own dirty work on the Relievers
Who even now are fighting down the fire—
But not the blazing Headlines of the Liar
That, once igniting, set the world ablaze
And rumble round the universe for days
In spite of experts and of the surviving
Inhabitants, on contradiction thriving:
But of these last, the vandals without pity
When they have time, before they leave a city,
Rounding them up, will drive them out before them
Though they have neither food nor housing for them,
Shooting the lame down, lest they should remain
To taste the life of liberated Spain.

[1] Englishmen's ears always go red in the Spanish sunlight.

Thus when in Alcaniz too swift we entered,
The young and old of Teruel were centred
Starving and cold:—and could not be shot down,
Because we came too quickly on the Town.
Weeping and laughing, as released from hell,
They kissed our hands and on our necks they fell,
With spectral looks, and ghastly tales to tell.
But always, as if blasé to their fate,
We catch some criminals who've lurked too late
Whether in drunken sleep, or, oft as not,
In cynical indifference to their lot,
As in this type, found hid in the latrine,
In whose great "Front" the "popular" is seen,
They've caught the "Mayor" escaping with his pelf,
Personified Democracy himself,
Who lately ran the tavern by the Gate
Till crime and cunning raised him to this state;
Searching his huge anatomy they find
A stick of dynamite (ensconced behind),
Type-written death-warrants, permits to plunder
And other rigmaroles of blood and thunder:
Of wads of money they unload his pockets
With filed-off rings, bracelets, and golden lockets,
And a fine crucifix of diamond sheen
To guy the fervour of some Touring Dean,
Till safely o'er the border he can shark it
To Perpignan, the Rhinos' plunder-market.
The angry crowd around him as he gapes
Accusing him of robberies and rapes
Would lynch him on the spot before a trial
Which granted him in spite of their denial,
Soon overwhelmed, they stew him in his slime
Of callousness, incompetence, and crime.
Oftener than not he'll ask to have a priest,
To die a Christian though he lived a beast,—
We granting heathens at their slightest fuss
The sacraments they still deny to us.
Safely confiding in our rules so strict
That sadism and torture interdict,
Sure of an easy death, a painless roll,

Without his own refineries to thole,
After his rage of blood and lust and pillage,
Thus ends the brief Vitellius of a village
With his best henchmen, such as can be found,
Stretched in their long siesta on the ground,
While industry unchained, puts forth his hand
And to its Mother-country draws the Land,
Food-lorries down the busy roadway lurch
And the first Mass is sounded from the Church,
The nerves of human confidence restored
To men at last, and glory to the Lord,
A sounding Fiat over chaos spread,
To the wronged justice, to the hungry bread,
And lasting vindication to the dead!
So from fierce Odyssies in foreign lands
Town after town returns to friendly hands
Like roaming prodigals come home to dine
On fatted calves from herding with the swine:
Thrown off its Russian smock of smoke and dirt,
Each village hustles on its fine Blue Shirt
Of cloudless heaven arrowed by the storks,
And turns to Spain its signpost at the forks,
Drives out its cows to graze with easy cheer,
And sees its pictured bugbears disappear
As schoolboys vanish at the master's cough:
Stalin and Lenin and Vorochiloff
In acres from the hoardings peeling off,
Like withered skins from blisters flayed away
Are blown about the fields in windy play:
While faded Kremlins to the pavement flop
And the Red Army, routed by the mop,
Gives place to Sunday's bullfight, flaring bold
With scarlet capes and uniforms of gold;
And, see, the Bullring to its use restored,
Where late the loud, half-hourly "Meeting," roared;
For every time the bolsheviks are routed,
Why, sure, a Meeting must be held about it,
Which held, and many resolutions passed,
They seek a bigger trouncing than the last,
And then a bigger meeting than the beating,

And so the endless rigmarole repeating,
From meeting to defeat, defeat to meeting,
From rout to rout so rapidly they switch
That nobody could tell you which was which.
We count our victories by meetings held—
And every time the Albert Hall is swelled
With democratic sympathy or ire,
We haul a county through the line of fire
Home to the azure roof of its desire.
When rooked by priests, of souls, which are his pelf,
The Devil holds a meeting to himself,
Clenches his lifted fist, emits a scream,
And lets off clouds of valuable steam,
Which we hold in, with silent lips compressed,
Conserving all our energy and zest,
Silent in outrage, silent in defeat,
But broad in laughter when the Charlies "meet";
Red Meetings are our very life and stay:
The cobble-stones to victory are they:
Blown Orators go home to sleep contented
Like Pickwick, when some harmless oath he'd vented.
Our business is to keep them to their tongues
And make our bellows of their working lungs
To blow our laughter to the merry fire
Which keeps them dithering with hate and ire—
The symptoms of Democracy decayed
And always to its enemies an aid;
Sanctions applied produced the same effect
Accelerating what they would have checked.
But worse than "Meetings" to the Red confusion,
And drawing on the war to its conclusion,
Felt in the air, and rising from the mould,
As found Napoleon's generals of old,
And Stalin too will feel ere he grows cold,
The hatred of the populace unsleeping
Which holds the final verdict in its keeping,
A silent force that, swelled from day to day,
Not half a million murders could allay,
Though terrorized, yet tacit in its spite
To see no undertaking works aright,

Sour scanted vintages bewray its wrongs,
Poor bread that was not harvested to songs
But reaped with silent curses in the mind,
Slack sinews, and a rifle-butt behind.
This is the *Land-hate*, knotted in the grass,
That trips the legs of armies as they pass,
So that the Reds dare never slip their rein—
One hand still busy with their captives' chain:
While we, with both hands free and forward face,
Need never look behind, as on we race,
And the freed country runs to our embrace;
As they must garrison what ground they take,
Beneath our feet new cohorts leap awake,
And sullen conscripts in their rear who ran
In ours become the tigers of the van;
Nor have they yet a single city taken
But level with the ground its walls were shaken,
While everywhere from Portugal to France
The population rose at our advance.
But their whole struggle, since the maiden shot,
Has been in hanging on to what they've got:
Step after step implacably reversed
Losing the All they started with at first
And might have kept had they but gently nursed
As they have fiercely brutalized and cursed:
No mercy, then, when all was in their powers!
And yet no whining on the part of ours—
And now they take their sob-stuff to the Deans,
And Barcelona apes the Picture-Queens;
Rivers of slime down painted cheeks she pumps,
Because we bounced her ammunition-dumps,
Deposed with cunning care where the crowds were quickest,
And praying for a hit where they were thickest,
Her cameras prepared on the veranda—
The cynic master-coup of propaganda—
She'll sponge our mercy to keep safe the squibs
Intended for our families and kids
As when they bathed Toledo in its gore
Before we hardly knew there was a war;
And when our pity breaks beneath the strain,

Revolted by Castellón's hundreds slain
Not by the chance of bombs or bursting shell,
But slain by hand, as when Bielsa fell,
Women and children massacred pell-mell
Lest they rejoice beneath our flag to dwell—
When we let off their subterranean dump
That settled half their city on its rump
And saved as much of ours at the same time
Though bombing ours, of course, is not a crime—
With tears and horror she laments the loss
Of those she brought the stick of bombs across.
The Devil take the pastoral Pamplona
But God preserve the bloody Barcelona—
Where all who are not anarchists or Reds
Were massacred or butchered in their beds!
But when the type that laid Toledo's mine,
The martyred crocodile, begins to whine,
Six hundred deaths arouse more indignation
Than sixty thousand by assassination:
One cut-throat being worth a hundred Spanish,
It does not matter how or when they vanish:
But hands off comrade cut-throat and his bleating,
Or they'll denounce you at the Wowsers' Meeting!
No blame for him is ever thought or said,
Who stores the bombs beneath his own wife's bed
Which he intends for ours: and so may bag
Three birds with one stone: rid him of his hag,
Worth more as propaganda than alive
When hungry mouths for failing rations strive:
Keep safe his bomb-dump while our patience lasts
While from its store our open towns he blasts,
Then, when his dump and wife are skyward hurled
To reap the sympathy of half the world,
Pass round the hat for sympathetic pence
Which never fail where limey's wits are dense,
While Chamberlain rebukes, and Blum protests,
For any one can bomb our open nests:
But powder magazines when "governmental"
Attain a value more than sacramental,
And holier than hospitals or shrines

244

Must be considered, when the Anarch whines.

Cooped in a trench, it was my chance to study,
My neighbour for a day or two, a bloody
Unburied arm, left lying in the snow
Which melted now its attitude to show,
Quite independent of its late discarder,
Clenching its fist on Nothing, clenching harder
Than to a stolen penny clings a child:
But to the desert scene unreconciled
That seemed so well to sympathize with it,
With knuckles so inextricably knit,
It seemed against the Universe to hit,
As it would storm and hammer at the sun
Knocking for entry till the world be done—
Yet with no guest to follow in behind
Should it an opening or a welcome find:
For now perhaps its widower begs for pence
In some far town, with humble deference,
And he it feeds may now be reconciled
To the new ears through which he is reviled
(For on a beggar "comrade" seldom smiled)
And so to peace of wisdom may have passed,
His world explained through suffering at last.
But here his fury is external yet
In frozen paroxysm fixed and set
Constricted on the Nothing in its hold
A clenched fist that Nothing can unfold
Nothing can satisfy, Nothing appease,
Though in its grasp that zeroid treasure freeze
And there is Nothing more for it to seize—
All that it wished to leave of the crushed world,
Compassed, and in its grip of lock-jaw curled—
And yet with its contorted boomerang
Of hate, it seemed my vigil to harangue
And on my mind, as on its table, bang,
As it were brandished by some unseen one
Who for a shape my fancy came to dun—
Which straight I gave, galvanic through the shoulder
Riving it to an orator to match,—

The portly bulk of the adjoining boulder
Whose grim ventriloquism I could catch
And in this hasty stenograph will match—
For so he cried, the world was growing colder:
And his volcanic language was of Matter,
Of atoms and electrons in revolt,
Who now had risen up the soul to shatter
And its Creator from his throne to jolt:—
For those that fought against us with such hate
Were negatives of us: by their disgust,
As we by love, engendered from the dust,—
"Men without God" it cried, "as I'm an arm
Without a man!" and as their will was harm
To all that wished not to partake their rage,
Out of creation would have torn the page
Of Adam's sin (whose load they scorn to heave),
And of the certain victory of Eve.
But having tried it—tearing like a sleeve,
The rebel arm, instead of what it clutched,
Broke off, and left the Eternal Law untouched.
Setting its owner free (and better maimed
Of a self-hurting member so inflamed)
With still one arm to beg its way, reclaimed
By sheer necessity: with open right hand
To take forgiveness for the clenched and tight hand
And all its bloody skill in working harms:
With five spread fingers yoking at the wrist
Become the emblem of the Falangist,[1]
With these, unused before, to take its alms:
And in the five yoked arrows of its bones
To radiate the grace that all atones,
Receiving silver bread for recent stones.

In the Sierra soars a silent cross
In a wild howl of solitude, where Loss

---

[1] The Falange has been called a Fascist organization. It was never that, as its founder pointed out in 1934, when he declined the invitation to attend the International Fascist Reunion. It has somewhat declined owing to its providing a convenient roosting place for turncoat Reds. During the war it was a Christian organization.

Is concrete; and a thing that's like a Cry
(But not of Gredos' wolves, nor of their ghosts,
Though these were myriad) fills the windless sky
At calmest noon, no less when thunders fly—
Waging its strife at those bleak, headlong coasts
We feel it rushing without sound or form—
A waterless Niagara, cloudless storm,
Or airless hurricane, that strips no pine
Nor stirs the frailest of the cloudy fleeces;
All that I know is that it never ceases,
Plangent, to rage, though with no outward sign:
Though Animal, its fury seems to be
That it is neither Dead, nor yet Divine:
It has not the sure measure of the sea
But rather the short pangs of giving Birth,
In anguish, to a monstrous, empty thing,
A world, perhaps, and vaster than this earth,
But hollow, and where hollow men complain:
It makes us think of human sperms: their King
Having Ascended, victory to gain,
And if those sperms behind him that remain,
Were magnified us men to represent—
Such would be their complaint and such their voice
Save that some few who witnessed His Ascent
And strove to follow in the way He went
Might curse their luck, but in His Own rejoice
And that give fire and courage to their breath,
While all the billion rest who failed the bliss
Might found a grim community of death
From which would rise some rumour such as this
Plangent and terrible from the abyss—
While He, the Victor, on his lonely Cross,
Unknown of them, rides like an Albatross
As here against the blue meridian sky;
To see that Eagle Aviator fly
And know there has been Triumph through our loss
Would be enough: though here upon the land
Like grimed mechanics we should have to stand
And watch: He sees our agony long-drawn,
The land unrolls its parchment with the dawn,

The long horizon tingles into pain
And like a distant grassfire on the plain,
The line of battle rolls along the sky
Where in His image fighting myriads die:
Like the two thieves on either side that hung
The one to Victory who clutched and clung,
Whose Life was started with his dying breath,
While the still-born with curses choked to Death.
To stop the tragedy so wild and grim
Fought to the Death for love or hate of Him
And soon to fill the world—what should with-hold
His hand but (as the whole created world
Were Sodom, or worse Barcelona) He
Should pull the lever and let fall the sun
To bomb the whole into oblivion,
Seeing that His own fierceness to Himself,
The anguish of His mother seven-times-sworded,
And her two thousand years of grief, by deaf
Ingratitude and sin were so rewarded:
But that her pity, boundless as our sin
Or as His strength—the yet unmeasured three
Whose trigon hems the Universe within,
The solar bounds of that exceeded sea;
But that her pity reaches to His arm,—
As it in strength, or as our sin in harm,
So great in mercy, terrible in charm,—
And holds it back, and tempers it with tears,
As ever for these last two thousand years:
And as with failing strength her pity clings,
Into his lifted hand the impulse springs
Of growing wrath that heats his aegis white,
Which balances betwixt her failing might,
His love, and the revenging will to smite
The cause of both his unhealed, bleeding scars,
And those redeeming tears, of Life the Spring;
And there he towers, the pilot of the stars,
Above the world, a cowed and guilty thing—
As a young airman furiously might wing
Above the town in which his bride was raped
And with his children murdered, like a king

Of vengeance, with his purpose fully shaped
To batter down its cursed walls in heaps,
Yet to his main objective turns his wing
And to the deed his anger cannot bring—
For there the Mother still survives and weeps.
Salve Regina! by whose love forfended
When every hope or remedy was lost
The fearful ultimatum was extended,
The ransom paid again with bitter cost!
Through Her the doom, deferred with saving pity,
Rumbled far off from the devoted city
Sparing the guilty walls for One within,
To strike, where first its havoc was intended,
The Central Plant and Arsenal of Sin:
While by her grace, her sufferings transcended,
With a new life and labour to begin,
Victorious Spain, the martyr, rose sublime
To stay the fatal avalanche of crime,
The suicidal landslide of man's soul
Which in contagious ruin drew the whole
Devoted race towards the foul morass;
And would have worked the huge collapse of time,
Its towers of history, and peaks of rhyme,
Into the spiral, infinite crevass—
Where even Deathly Satan scorns to pass
While yet from Her he gets a wage to skivvy on
(Who for some time yet has his work to do
For fear security should rot us through)
Preferring Hell to such abject Oblivion,
Being of a nobler line than me or you.
He never backed this infra-human chute
Which has no part in devil, fiend or brute
But came as much from disbelief in him
As godlessness—Negation, vast, and grim,
And absolute, of all save honest Matter
Who at the unwonted worship paid to him
Of the whole universe the humblest limb,
Gets shy at first, then madder than a hatter,
And lays about, these godless thugs to shatter,
With their own economics and mechanics

Throwing his own supporters into panics,
Cuckolding pedantry with its own science
To breed from that irregular alliance
Rebellious cyclopses and laughing giants
Who'll fight in any cause but dull statistics'
And seem most snug amidst the Unattainable,
Performing in the legions of the mystics
Impossibilities, and unexplainable—
No, not gymnastics—call them Falangistics!
For Matter has opinions of its own
As any one who's worked with wood or stone
Can tell you, or who swims or flies or rows—
It has to be caressed by one who knows!
Reluctantly it fights with its Creator,
But turns its wrath upon the agitator,
And sure the Devil prays both day and night
Knowing no prayers are hopeless in Her sight
For even he some fleeting hope may feel
To escape the final pension of her heel—
To see so many shameless thugs ashamed,
So many brutes to honesty reclaimed
Forgetful and forgiven of their crime.
Which unheard miracles bespeak a time
When there'll be even hope to burst their fetters
For the most abject souls on earth who dwell,
Bawds, child-defilers, ponces, men of letters,
Those who for foreign gold their countries sell
With intellectuals and what more foul
And dirty in its ragged womb may howl,
Since even I such grace of her have won
And of the Dawn in Europe seen the Sun,—
Heart of the Human Phoenix newly born
From his own blood—for nothing on this earth
Except through sacrifice had fruitful birth
Or it was blood that reddened for its morn;
Lit furnace in the heart of the New Man,
New because older than this world outworn
Whose broken shell his energy has torn
With phoenix plumes the burning Truth to fan
That centuries of liberals forgot,

Chained to the world as to a trundling shot
By the lewd belly and the itching sex
With the sun's scornful brand around their necks
For heavy satisfaction to besot—
Who gasp to see their age-to-finish fort
For laughing hurricanes the crazy sport,
And through its snuggest sun-defying holes,
The Glory fox those communizing souls
That on our own would force their godless lot,
By fire and torture, in like holes to rot:
But now for mercy howl with sagging knees
That lately were for toasting us like cheese—
Mercy be granted: but no more asleep
Let the bright sword be caught within its sheath
By lurking crocodiles that watch beneath,
Azañas and Prietos of the deep,
Still to the triple chin the point of steel
Be kept, the eyes with vigilance afire
When any new Vitellius would aspire
To drag our virgins at his bloody heel:
Be thou O solar heart the joyous wheel
On which we grind its scintillating steel
And Lightning in the Right Hand of the Killer
Be the blue sword, and to the Dragon death,
Wherever he would spew his venomed breath
Against the Virgin Nike of the Pillar!
The Winged Victory of Earth and Sky,
Before whose might the godless legions cower,
Their terror praising what they most deny
And came with fire and torture to devour.

Her beauty like a cream-white bronca rearing
To snort her flame-red hurricane of hair,
For the first time to mortal eyes appearing
That were not vowed to innocence or prayer;
Whose heart exposed, and through its wounds so gory,
As from a distant battleship at night,
Raying the searchlights of eternal glory,
Bombarded us with thunderbolts of love
As we rushed on to storm the heights above:

For it was She that burning on to France
Unfurled the splendid signal to advance
When in the stars our sacred ensign shone[1]
And like a comet through the tempest trailing
Her stormy hair, along the skyline sailing,
With red and golden banner waved us on:
While at the portent blazing over Spain,
The Heavens seemed with blood and fire to rain,
And at the sight, the foe, half-dead with fright,
Fled howling in their Gadarene stampede,
Nor stop to help their comrades when they bleed
But downwards to the ocean hurl their flight,
And shed their arms, in mountains, on the plain,
Who still that we are better armed complain
When it is due to their careering speed,
Who leave more armaments than we would need
Were the whole War twice over to be won!
So once again the soul-destroying horde
That first with Attila its frenzy roared
And now the living world had overrun,
Has howled and fled before the Christian sword
Of Spain; though never in so vast a plan
Was massed the whole pathology of man
In Freudian delirium made one
By bestial deeds that horrify the sun.
So spoke a legionary to his gun,
Whose silence sounded sweet as a guitar
Out on the plain, beneath the evening star.
Next morning came the swallows on the wing,
And the long war was finished by the Spring.

As flowered the Ocean, at Dione's birth,
But to a prouder footfall, foams the Earth.
While peach and cherry crash through broken walls
Like breakers on the piers with flying shawls,
White almond-groves dissolve in showers of spray,
Spume of the winds and starlight of the day,

[1] The Red and Yellow aurora borealis that waved, over the battlefield
at Alfambra, the authentic colours of Spain, when the Reds, thinking it
a "secret weapon" broke, fled, and never stopped till they reached the sea.

To nebulise the noon and shoal the sward
With Milky Ways a fetlock in the ford.
To float the wingèd Nike home to Spain
And launch her on the waving seas of grain,
The Spring with rosy spinnaker outfanned
Comes curling silver fleeces through the land.
And now the Sun his fragrant camp disposes
Field-Marshal of the battlefields of roses,
Where, mitrailleuse of song, each nightingale
Triggers upon a thorn her sounding flail
To shower those diamonds of refulgent hail,
As if to thresh a gem from every flake
Where swirling petals snow their drifted lake,
With full heart fusillading through the hours,
Whose shots are gems, whose smoke the scent of flowers,
Whose bursts are soaring raptures that she hurls
With pollen for her powder, firing pearls!
   As when a shot rings through the Nubian lakes
The white shores, shimmering into scarlet flakes,
Take wing for twenty leagues, and, all as one,
Revolving rise and kindle in the sun—
The lit flamingoes soar in widening rings
And raise a second sunrise with their wings . . .
   So she, the Wingèd Victory of our hosts,
With harmony uplifts our burning ghosts,
As if our souls were swirling drifts of flowers
From which the lit hosannas rain in showers,
Threshed by the level rays, like driven sleet,
To flash in pearls and rubies round her feet,
Where tears and blood-drops, turned to gems divine,
In wheeling galaxies revolve and shine,
By martyrs shed, two hundred thousand strong,
With all the sky a cyclone to their song!
So Greco saw her rise above this town
With whistling gales of azure for her gown,
Where rainbows pulse as in the Arctic blaze,
Or through a dolphin's scales the volted rays—
To make at last the Mystery appear
Flame to the eye, and trumpet to the ear,
How Eve should stand within the starry wheel

With the foul serpent writhing at her heel,
Whose hydra heads subside through all the land,
Who throws his last convulsions on the sand
To farrow forth his latest spawn of Lies
Abortively to crawl to Northern skies—
Though harmless here, where, as in Saturn's rings,
The charmèd circles of delight she flings
On every side, with flushed, auroral wings,
Whose spokes, at last, unite their myriad hue
Till sight, itself, the radiance must subdue
To form this stainless aquiline of blue,
This sky, that veils so rapturous a thing,
Like sunlight through a passing eagle's wing,
Lest our whole being should become one Eye,
And our sole will—to suffer, bleed, and die!

Now every heart's a calyx or a lyre
Or censer lit with self-consuming fire,
And even in the breath that we respire,
Faint wafts of frost, from far-off peaks of snow,
Ignite and tremble with a rosy glow,
A fiery nimbus, fuming ferns of gold,
Fresh to exhale as lovely to behold—
My horse and I, who else in shade were lost,
Four ostrich-feathers burning through the frost
Under huge shades of colonnading oak
Whose shadows fall, as from an axe's stroke,
Gigantic from the horizontal rays
Across a league-wide valley, white with sprays.
   Then by the river's city-skirting tide
Around the Moorish battlements we ride
Faint-streaming through the shade of ivied walls,
Where light as from a foreign country falls
As through the loopholed buttresses it leaks,
Where jasmine clings, like thunder to the peaks,
Or makes a dewy starlight with its shade
Where through the noon the gloaming is delayed.

But where the more celestial gardens grow
Beyond the crystal chandeliers of snow,

Thorning his breast upon a tusk of ice,
A nightingale in rapture, breathing spice,
A swan in hue, expiring as he sings,
A phoenix in the fulgence of his wings,
The Sun himself consumes a richer pyre
With clouds for cinders, bleeding scented fire,
And pours the ashes of his flowery slaughter
To foam in gold along the rose-red water,
Wherein the Eagle City steeps her towers
Besieged by the aroma of her flowers,
While, like Veronica, the Tagus sweeps,
And on her flood the dear reflection keeps.
There mirrored in the water upside down,
She laves the poison'd spittle from her crown
Which Jews and Saxons squirt in Parthian flight
From inky glands, the loligos of spite—
With ruins in the freshening water sunk
To cleanse the tail-shot of the human skunk,
For Hell itself the deed with dirt must sign
To prove her queenly titles are divine;
And hers to none in history shall yield,
Where Christ the sword, and Mary was the shield,—
Lepanto, or the Catalaunian Field!
For here the Tartar's dreams were put to flight,
And Europe rescued in her own despite.
    With turrets turned to deep artesian wells
Where submarine cathedrals ring their bells,
A lotus in each loophole seems to flower
Where late the maxim hailed its deadly shower,
While irises in every crater show
And stars replace them when they cease to glow.
She seems with blooms and perfumes to rehearse
The Saga she commanded from my verse.
For see the lilies that for flames aspire
To take her ramparts with redeeming fire,
With spring to capture, and with buds reclaim
What Earthquake, Fire, or Thunder could not tame,
Vulcan beneath, or Jupiter above—
Capitulating to the touch of Love!

Down the grey gorge, the Tagus, burning red,
Circles the Eagle City with its fire.
The Requetés[1] their rosary have said:
The Angelus rings out from every spire:
And from its height, among its sister-cones
The mountain, with its garrison of stones,
With husky echo carries on the choir.
The Virgin of the Valley, watched the town
Above the headlong river looking down,
Upon whose flood reflected angels soar
In flames of blood to skim the liquid ore,
Where swallows must descend to kiss those skies
To which their matchless wings can never rise
Except by stooping downwards to adore.

[1] Carlist soldiers.